THE OLDER BROTHER RETURNS

"I read the book initially as a pat... ...e scalpel of an expert surgeon. The story ...ayers of accumulated rationalizations ov... ... in me the hardness and judgmental atti... ...brother. I based a retreat week on the material o... ...d I repented over and over as I found new freedom in ... a firm commitment to change into a compassionate and merciful father."

— FR. MICHAEL SCANLAN, T.O.R.
from the Foreword

"Neal Lozano has achieved a valuable set of reflections on a series of problems which plague not only Christian communities like Neal's, but which are at the base of many of the difficulties real people have with living the Christian life in today's society."

— MSGR. THOMAS J. HERRON, S.S.L., S.T.D.
Saint Charles Borromeo Seminary

"For those of us who feel the pressure or have succumbed to the influences of our modern religious culture, this book offers a fresh perspective and a positive encouragement."

— DONALD L. BARTEL
serving with The Navigators

"Neal's book is devoted to analyzing the dynamics of the older brother found within all of us. It is an original and sensitive contribution to the literature of spiritual growth and holiness that will be helpful to many."

— RALPH MARTIN
Renewal Ministries

The
Older
Brother
Returns

Neal Lozano

**Finding a Renewed Sense
of God's Love and Mercy**

The Attic Studio Press

CLINTON CORNERS, NEW YORK

Grateful acknowledgment is made to Ruth Whiston Upshall and the
Whiston family for permission to use "The Peanut Brittle Story,"
first published in *Are You Fun to Live With?* by Lionel Whiston
(1895-1994), copyright © 1968 by Life Enrichment Publishers.

The names of some persons have been changed.

THE OLDER BROTHER RETURNS

Published by

THE ATTIC STUDIO PRESS
P.O. BOX 75
CLINTON CORNERS, NY 12514

Phone: 845–266–8100
E–mail: AtticStudioPress@aol.com

Cover and book design by Joseph (Trip) Sinnott
PRINTED IN THE UNITED STATES OF AMERICA

04 05 06 07 5 4 3 2

Library of Congress Cataloging-in-Publication Data

Lozano, Neal, 1949–
    The older brother returns : finding a renewed sense of God's
love and mercy / Neal Lozano.
        p.   cm.
    ISBN 1-883551-51-X (alk. paper)
    1. Prodigal son (Parable)—Criticism, interpretation, etc.
2. Spiritual life—Catholic Church. 3. God—Love. 4. God—Mercy.
5. God—Worship and love. 6. Catholic Church—Doctrines.
    I. Title.
BT378.P8L69   1995
226.8'06—dc20   95-41024
                                                  CIP

Dedication

TO THE
NEXT GENERATION
OF
PRODIGALS

Contents

Foreword

THE PARABLE KNOWN AS The Prodigal Son has been a
seemingly inexhaustible treasure to be rediscovered and
brought forth in every age. In this book, Neal Lozano chroni-
cles an exciting application of the parable as it focuses on the
elder son.

I read the book initially as a patient coming under the
scalpel of an expert surgeon. The story cut through many lay-
ers of accumulated rationalizations over the years to expose
in me the hardness and judgmental attitude of an older
brother. I based a retreat week on the material of the book
and I repented over and over as I found new freedom in making a firm commitment to change into a compassionate and
merciful father.

Indeed, the parable itself has been better labeled The
Merciful Father, for indeed the focus and teaching of the
parable is not how people get in trouble and become lost but
rather how the loving and merciful Father receives them back
with great joy. Nevertheless, the hidden treasure of the parable lies in the new ways in each age that those who once
belonged to the Father's household can leave home—through
physical separation and activity as with the younger son, or
through withdrawal of the heart as with the older son.

The older brother is not truly at home with his father. He rejects his brother and resents any love or favor going out to him. He wants the father's respect and blessings but doesn't want the father's heart. He has lost the joy of living in the father's house and withdraws his heart to a self-centered and proud realm. He ends up in the parable standing outside the house while his brother enjoys the celebration within.

For every reader this book will touch a note of realism that will engender both a healthy caution against older brother attitudes as well as sympathy for the zealous ones who fall into the older brother trap. These are lessons that can only be partly learned though analysis. The real power of the lesson comes from walking through the story. This book gives each of us that opportunity.

I have watched the author develop as a mature Catholic Christian since his high school days. I introduced him to Catholic Charismatic Renewal and stood on the side as a resource, friend and relative as he led the founding of a Christian community. I had the privilege of presiding at his wedding and the baptisms of his children. I can attest to his high level of integrity, solid Christian character and a wisdom developed from prayer, study, and that purification which comes from responsible leadership. The fruit of this character development is evident to all who read this penetrating and freeing book.

— REV. MICHAEL SCANLAN, T.O.R.
Steubenville, Ohio

The Parable

*T*HERE WAS A MAN *who had two sons. The younger one said to his father, "Father, give me my share of the estate." So he divided his property between them.*

Not long after that, the younger son got together all he had, set off for a distant country and there squandered his wealth in wild living. After he had spent everything, there was a severe famine in that whole country, and he began to be in need. So he went and hired himself out to a citizen of that country, who sent him to his fields to feed pigs. He longed to fill his stomach with the pods that the pigs were eating, but no one gave him anything.

When he came to his senses, he said, "How many of my father's hired men have food to spare, and here I am starving to death! I will set out and go back to my father and say to him: Father, I have sinned against heaven and against you. I am no longer worthy to be called your son; make me like one of your hired men." So he got up and went to his father. But while he was still a long way off, his father saw him and was filled with compassion for him; he ran to his son, threw his arms around him and kissed him.

The son said to him, "Father, I have sinned against heaven and against you. I am no longer worthy to be called your son."

But the father said to his servants, "Quick! Bring the best robe and put it on him. Put a ring on his finger and sandals on his feet. Bring the fattened calf and kill it. Let's have a feast and celebrate. For this son of mine was dead and is alive again; he was lost and is found." So they began to celebrate.

Meanwhile, the older son was in the field. When he came near the house, he heard music and dancing. So he called one of the servants and asked him what was going on. "Your brother has come," he replied, "and your father has killed the fattened calf because he has him back safe and sound."

The older brother became angry and refused to go in. So his father went out and pleaded with him. But he answered his father, "Look! All these years I've been slaving for you and never disobeyed your orders. Yet you never gave me even a young goat so I could celebrate with my friends. But when this son of yours who has squandered your property with prostitutes comes home, you kill the fattened calf for him!"

"My son," the father said, "you are always with me, and everything I have is yours. But we had to celebrate and be glad, because this brother of yours was dead and is alive again; he was lost and is found." (Luke 15:11-32)

1

Where Do I Fit in the Story?

LATE HAVE I LOVED YOU! YOU WERE WITHIN ME,
AND I WAS IN THE WORLD OUTSIDE MYSELF. ...
YOU WERE WITH ME. BUT I WAS NOT WITH YOU.

— Saint Augustine, *Confessions*

FOR SIXTEEN YEARS a large banner has hung on the wall above our dining room table. The scene is an embracing father and son. Every day that depiction of the Prodigal Son's return home reminds me of the heavenly Father's love for his children. It reminds me of my own journey as a wayward son welcomed into the Father's arms.

For a long time I viewed this parable as a story about the lost son, the character I most identified with.

THE PRODIGAL COMES HOME

As A HIGH SCHOOL AND college student I had wandered away from "home." My lifestyle had become incompatible with my Christian upbringing. More and more, I lived for weekends, which meant parties, drinking, and "fun." Then in 1969, during my junior year at Villanova University, my father died. With his passing, I experienced a profound sense of emptiness and meaninglessness about life. I went looking for answers.

Six months after my father's death, I sat in the den of my own home and asked my cousin, a priest, to explain the Mass to me. I was wondering if I could find some meaning in it. To my surprise, Fr. Mike did not present any deep insightful thoughts about the Eucharist. He simply turned to me and said, "Unless you go into church knowing God, you'll never understand what it's all about."

In that moment a deep awareness came upon me. *I have no faith.* Yet there was also a protest from within. *How can this be? I was raised in the church. I was an altar boy. My parents were prayerful and had a deep faith. How could this be?*

As these thoughts swirled in my head, my cousin suggested we pray together. Not waiting for a response, he began, "Father, here I am with Neal whom I love."

That's strange, I thought, *he's speaking to God as if God were a person. That's kind of nice.* Then he asked the Holy Spirit to come, and at that moment I experienced the new life that Jesus has promised to those who believe.

To me this was miraculous. I'd never realized anyone could personally encounter the Lord. Sure, I knew God was real. But now I found myself in a situation that seemed ridiculously funny. As I looked around, holding back my laughter, I thought, *God is in my den!*

I didn't fully understand what had happened to me that day in January 1970. I didn't have a teacher or a pastor to help, nor did I as yet feel at home or accepted in the church. Yet I knew that the reality of what I had encountered would change my life for good; I would never go back to life apart from the Lord. I was the prodigal come home! The party had begun. The fatted calf had been slain. I had found in Christ the meaning and purpose of my life.

I was in danger though, for I understood very little of what had been so generously given to me. Jesus said, "When anyone hears the message about the kingdom and does not understand it, the evil one comes and snatches away what was sown in his heart" (Matt. 13:19). In many ways I misunderstood or misinterpreted the meaning of that moment of homecoming. My first enthusiastic response had been, *I'll never feel lonely again. Everybody will want to know what I know. All my problems are over.* I wanted the feelings of that moment to be the reality of my life. I didn't know that Jesus is the reality, and the feelings are simply a response. I didn't realize that seeking God's kingdom is the pursuit of a lifetime.

THE OLDER BROTHER EMERGES

I CAME TO SEE the parable of the Prodigal Son as one of the most powerful stories in the Bible. That's why the banner hung for so many years in my dining room. But in recent years I've come to see the story more broadly than the prodigal's tale. It is really a family's tale—of a father's love for two sons, very different from each other. One child is a lost son come home, the other a seemingly faithful son who looms on the sidelines of this story. In recent years, I've been more and more concerned with the older brother in this parable. He has a story of his own, and in many ways it is my story since my 1970 return home.

For several years as a young Christian, I continually returned as a prodigal—in deeper repentance to the Lord, turning from my overt sins of the past. Over time the particular expressions of sin that initially exposed my emptiness— the drinking, cheating, lying and immoral relationships—had disappeared. And compared to those obvious sins, my current activities apart from the Lord seemed insignificant.

In 1971, after graduating from Villanova, I traveled to Ann Arbor, Michigan, and visited the emerging Word of God Community where young, zealous, radically committed Christians gathered to live together as a body to serve the Lord Jesus. On that trip God planted a vision in my heart for community life. Why couldn't we "do community" back in Philadelphia?

The vision for community wasn't that everyone would live together or have everything in common, but that there would be strong, committed relationships. Families and singles from diverse backgrounds would share together as followers of Jesus, serving one another in the unity of the Spirit.

But over the next three years my efforts to establish a community came to nothing. I longed to move away to a larger, more established community. That didn't work either; in my heart I knew that it was not what the Lord wanted for me.

During this time we laid the groundwork for a small community, eventually called the House of God's Light. Shortly after my wife Janet and I had the first of our four sons, we began sharing a house with a few singles from our university prayer group. Then a married couple from the group moved in across the street, and others wanted to join us. After one year of this informal community life, we moved into a larger house together: two married couples, one child, five singles—all very young, untrained, and inexperienced. Inspired by what we had seen in other communities and, I believe, led by the Holy Spirit, we sought to love the Lord and one another. We learned a great deal about what it means to live together, to forgive, and to work through difficulties.

I look back fondly on that initial year. It makes me consider the mercy of God and his willingness to allow his children to mess up even as they are on the way to becoming what he would have them be.

Finally, a year and a half later, we made a covenant. We knew that we would not all continue living in the same residence, but we had a deep desire to continue following God's call in our lives. Believing that God had a purpose in joining us together, we committed ourselves to be faithful to what he had done among us.

With all that we were doing to grow in community life, we were sliding, unbeknownst to us, into what I would call the "**older brother syndrome.**"

As I've looked at the banner hanging on my wall, I've imagined seeing the older brother in the background (he's not actually in the scene) looking on. Sure, he's standing firmly in his father's estate (he would never consider leaving), but he's not party to the intimate embrace. His face reveals an emptiness, an inner void that keeps him separated from the celebration in the front yard.

The older brother is the one who sees all that he has done but fails to see what is missing inside. "Look! All these years I've been slaving for you and never disobeyed your orders" (Luke 15:29). It is a subtle trap to fall in love with what God has done, rather than to love the One who has and is continually doing new things in our lives. To subtly or unknowingly forsake our first love is to fall into the older brother syndrome that traps us as individuals and drains movements, communities, and churches.

The older brother in the parable remained at home doing what he was told, but his heart had grown cold. His routine had become his life. We were faithfully doing what we perceived we were given to do—build Christian community. Yet something was missing inside. The task of building community had become a routine more important than our love for our Father.

Eventually, we found ourselves facing a critical issue in our community life. *Were we going to face the older brother in us and our need to embrace our Lord or were we going to ignore the grace God was giving us to repent?* Things on the surface were good. We could have clung to the way things were, trying to play it safe by holding on to what we had, or we could take a chance and begin again. I am convinced that if we had not faced the older brother in us, we would not be a community today.

And we have survived. Though many faces have changed, we are still a community of about a hundred people seeking to love and serve the Lord as his own people, joined together as brothers and sisters in Christ. We are a gathering of Catholics and Protestants, faithful to our traditions and church commitments, while also seeking to be faithful to the mission the Lord has given us as a community.

THE HUNGRY HEART

PERHAPS YOU REMEMBER a time that you had an encounter with the Lord and moved out with great enthusiasm and zeal, only to lose that zeal through difficulties and disillusionment. Or perhaps you experienced the Lord's direction and presence as you became part of a local body, a church, a prayer group, a community, or a religious order. Perhaps you joined a missionary work, a devotional group, a pro-life group, a ministry to the poor, or another Christian movement. Perhaps through disappointment and failure you now find yourself in a rut.

We all go through periods of loss of zeal and weakening of vision. God brings us into trials because he wants us to come to him. He wants more for us than living better lives; he wants us to share in his very life. He wants us to be in the Father's house and to enjoy the embrace of his loving arms. Through the prophet Amos, the Lord declared: "I gave you empty stomachs in every city and lack of bread in every town, yet you have not returned to me" (Amos 4:6). God gave them empty stomachs because he loved them and wanted more for them.

This book is not about Christian community. It is about life in Christ. It is about things we all share in common as we seek to be faithful to God's call to us. It is about the older brother in all of us—and may be of particular benefit to those who have lost their zeal and vision or have found their group stuck, unable to get moving again.

The story of the prodigal is as important to me today as it was when I was the wayward prodigal returning. I have actually been both brothers, more recently the older, the one who couldn't comprehend how a loving father could lavish an inheritance on an irresponsible child and then release that child (without a fight) to live recklessly. Like the older brother, I've been proud of my faithful service and obedience, judgmental of others who didn't live up to my—our community's—standards, more fearful of the opinions and judgments of others than of God, and needing to be in control of others and the environment. I no longer trusted in God's love but chose to work, to take my inheritance and do something with it. The good work I was doing for the Father—with a sincere desire to please him—had become corrupt.

WOULD WE WELCOME THE LOST SON?

OUR GENERATION, like every other, is full of "lost sons." Many of our children are leaving home in rebellion, and many Christians are falling to their knees, praying that the prodigals will return. And that prayer is the very cry and anguish of the waiting Father—finding its expression in us.

But this book is not about what God is doing to bring the lost home. It is about what God is doing among the older brothers—getting his family ready to receive the returning prodigals.

I have often wondered: *What would have happened if the prodigal had met his older brother instead of his father on the way back home?* Would the older brother have spewed out his resentment and bitterness? Would the younger brother have come under condemnation and turned away, feeling hopelessly unworthy? Would he have heard his brother's demand for justice and left again, utterly discouraged?

What will happen to the prodigals of this generation—our children—if they return to the church of Christ, the family of God, and don't find the Spirit of Christ waiting to embrace them? Will we as children of God be ready with forgiveness, generosity, and celebration? Will we be willing to accommodate them? Will we really value their return? Will we understand that the primary issue is not how they lived, what they have done, how they will fit in, how much their return inconveniences our routines, how much care they need . . . but simply that they were dead and now they are alive? Will we be willing to embrace them? Just as the onlookers unbound Lazarus after Jesus had raised him from the dead, will we be willing to unbind those whom Jesus has spiritually raised from the dead?

A friend of mine came to know the Lord during the Jesus People revival of the 60's, when an estimated eighty-five thousand young people were converted in a brief span of time. In the twenty-five years since, this man—devoted to and serving the Lord—has never found a church-community home. Whenever he goes to join a church, he runs into the "older brother" tending the door, and it inevitably doesn't work.

I mention my friend's story not to excuse him from his responsibility (for in some places he hasn't stayed because he has run into the older brother in himself). But his story makes me wonder: *How many more of those young people never really found their way into the Father's family?*

Indeed, I believe the Holy Spirit is grieving over the church, longing for the body of Christ to become more like the Father's house, and less like a haven for older brothers.

When I first came to Christ, I knew I was a prodigal. I had tasted of the glory of God. I had experienced his unconditional acceptance. Yet I quickly became the older brother, even as I still identified myself with the younger brother having returned home. May I invite you to discover where you fit in the story of the prodigal and the older brother—and open yourself to receive the Father's heart?

2

God's Revealing Light

JESUS GIVES US TO UNDERSTAND THAT WHAT HE
MEANS IN THE FIGURE OF THE ELDER BROTHER IS
THE TYPE OF PHARISEE WHO TAKES HIS ETHICAL
AND RELIGIOUS DUTIES IN BITTER EARNEST.

— Helmut Thielicke, *The Waiting Father*

SINS OF THE HEART

A BOUT NINETEEN YEARS AGO, when our community was
still very young, I felt the Lord speak to me. As I was
in prayer, an image came to my mind. It was a picture of a
huge tree stump which, at first glance, appeared to be dead.
But as I looked more closely, I could see that it was very
much alive, with a deep root system. Its "life" was out of
sight, primarily beneath the earth's surface.

What was the message I received? That this stump was a
picture of religious pride. And I realize now that that
glimpse—of an extensive, underground, entwined root sys-

tem—was the beginning of my understanding that something was wrong with my life and our community.

Something wrong? When "you can count on us" could have been our community slogan? Faithful. Loyal. Dependable. And as for myself personally, I was praying for an hour or more a day, serving the Lord, attending charismatic conferences, reading solid material, even teaching solid doctrine, and edifying the larger group.

If there was one thing the older brother had going for him it was his obedience. He "did what needed to be done." He looked righteous.

But something wasn't right in his heart.

In the Scriptures, the word *heart* refers to the center of a person, the place where deep conviction flows. The word encompasses more than the emotions, affections, and desires; it also includes the reason and the will.

I think of the prophet Samuel looking over the sons of Jesse, discerning which one the Lord had chosen to be Israel's next king. When Samuel inquired about Jesse's oldest son— the obvious choice—the Lord's word was clear: "Do not consider his appearance or his height. . . . The Lord does not look at the things man looks at. Man looks at the outward appearance, but the Lord looks at the heart" (1 Sam. 16:7).

God was not looking for the obvious good qualities. He was not looking for someone who was "picture perfect," with great talent, wisdom, and strength. He wanted a person who had a heart like God's.

The prophet Jeremiah said, "The heart is deceitful above all things" (Jer. 17:9). The Gospel accounts show Jesus spending considerable energy talking to the religious leaders of his day, religious leaders who did not hear or take kindly to what he was saying about sins of the heart. His primary concern was not their outward actions—their seeming righteousness—but what they were hiding behind their whitewashed exteriors.

SEARCH ME, O GOD

ONE DAY SEVERAL YEARS AGO, while praying outside a clinic, my heart broke as I watched a young girl walk inside the building to have an abortion. I sought God earnestly, praying that she would remember any past Christian training she'd had as a child, asking that she would be aware of the love of Jesus. *Oh, that his love would constrain her to turn away from this deadly deed.*

But as I prayed, the Lord convicted me that *my* sin was no different from hers. Every time I looked at a woman with lust in my heart, every time I lingered, allowing my affection and desire to be drawn to that which is not holy, I was casting a vote for the kingdom of darkness. Every time I disregarded God's authority over my life and went my own way because I thought I knew best, I was cooperating with the spirit of this age. I was in agreement with the thief who "comes only to steal and kill and destroy" (John 10:10), and the power that dulls our minds to the value of life. The sins of my heart were in agreement with the power of darkness—and therefore I had my own part in this baby's death.

Before King David died, he exhorted his son Solomon to acknowledge God and to serve him with wholehearted devotion. "The Lord searches every heart," David said, "and understands every motive behind the thoughts" (1 Chron. 28:9).

And the Lord who searches our hearts wants to expose our sin for what it is. Why? So he can redeem it. So he can enjoy an intimate relationship with us. You see, those rooted sins keep us from having an intimate relationship with our Father. They keep us in the older brother stance—living in the father's household but not relishing the warmth of his embrace. And the warmth of that embrace, the intimate relationship, is the inheritance God has for us.

In Psalm 139 David again speaks of how deeply and intimately God knows us—God our Creator, the One who knit us together in our mother's womb. At the end of the psalm David makes a request of the Lord: "Search me, O God, and know my heart; test me and know my anxious thoughts. See if there is any offensive way in me, and lead me in the way everlasting" (vv. 23-24).

If we want to break out of the older brother syndrome, we need to start with the spirit of this psalm: "Search me, O God." We must give God permission to reveal the truth to us.

It is my prayer that God will use the lessons shown to our community and discussed in these pages to speak to others about the older brother syndrome, its hidden traps, temptations, and deceptions.

Conversion doesn't come through study alone; our primary need is for revelation. It is the truth that sets us free. As we ask God for wisdom, he will give it. When we seek his help, recognizing our individual and corporate dependence on him, he will expose deception by the light of his truth.

But while it is important to understand ourselves, this cannot be our primary focus. To make our hearts, our weakness, or our sin the focus of our attention is to lose the power of the Holy Spirit to wash us. We end up working on ourselves in futility. The focus of our desire, the yearning of our souls, must be to see Christ, to know the Father and embrace him who first loved us—as we did when we were prodigals returning to him from our wanton ways.

"BUT HOW CAN GOD BRING THIS ABOUT IN ME?" LET HIM DO IT, AND PERHAPS YOU WILL KNOW HOW.

— George Macdonald, *Unspoken Sermons*

3

Living Beyond Legalism

LOOK! ALL THESE YEARS I'VE BEEN SLAVING FOR
YOU AND NEVER DISOBEYED YOUR ORDERS.

— The older brother

A TEENAGER'S FREEDOM

NOW THAT I HAVE teenagers of my own, I often find
myself thinking back to my own youth—to the time
when I was finally in high school. To me this meant freedom
to spend more time with my peers, freedom from the restrictions and rules of childhood.

But I didn't anticipate the new restrictions set by peer
pressure. Being part of their group meant I lived in line with
their group rules. I had a friend who seemed to know all the
rules—the right way to dress, which girls were good looking,
which words were cool and which were not. I was never sure
how he knew all these things, but I stuck near him so I could
glean even the smallest grains of his knowledge. Of course, I
couldn't ask him questions outright. This would have

revealed my ignorance and jeopardized my right to belong to the in-group.

Keep in mind that this scenario is depicting my world of "freedom"—freedom to be part of a group, the best group. I knew there were serious deficiencies in every other group in the school.

I also knew that wearing baggy pants to school would be a most humiliating death—almost as bad as when I had joined the swim club and gone to the pool wearing a bathing suit that was, well, unique (i.e., different from what everyone else was wearing).

I didn't know much about fashion. (I still don't. My wife and children keep me well informed.) All I knew in 1963 was that tight pants were better than baggy and that short pants—showing off your white socks—were better than long pants touching your shoes.

One day a friend and I went to the store—without my mother. I quickly and surreptitiously picked out a pair of pants that were a bit on the tight and short side. The clerk told me they might shrink. *But what if they didn't?* I just couldn't take the risk of buying a bigger size. Of course they did shrink and became uncomfortable, and, at that age, within six weeks I had grown enough so that I couldn't force myself into them. The process then started all over again: buying a new pair of pants that would fit me, but not for long.

THE FIRST-CENTURY CHURCH

NOW LET ME TURN to a New Testament story with a thread and weave that may look familiar. First let's set the scene, in Jerusalem:

All the believers were one in heart and mind. No one claimed that any of his possessions was his own, but they shared everything they had. With great power the apostles continued to testify to the resurrection of the Lord Jesus, and much grace was upon them all. There were no needy persons among them. For from time to time those who owned lands or houses sold them, brought the money from the sales and put it at the apostles' feet, and it was distributed to anyone as he had need. (Acts 4:32-35)

What a wonderful time in the history of the church. The presence of the Holy Spirit moved the community of believers to extraordinary generosity and selflessness. Without programs and fund raising and budgets and constitutions, the needy were cared for. On occasion, someone was led to sell property and give it away. But flowing from this great gift of the Lord to the believers is the first recorded account of sin in the early church.

Now a man named Ananias, together with his wife Sapphira, also sold a piece of property. With his wife's full knowledge he kept back part of the money for himself, but brought the rest and put it at the apostles' feet. Then Peter said, "Ananias, how is it that Satan has so filled your heart that you have lied to the Holy Spirit and have kept for yourself some of the money you received for the land? Didn't it belong to you before it was sold? And after it was sold, wasn't the money at your disposal? What made you think of doing such a thing? You have not lied to men but to God." When Ananias heard this, he fell down and died. And great fear seized all who heard what had happened. Then the young men came forward, wrapped up his body, and carried him out and buried him. About three hours later his wife came in, not knowing what had happened. Peter asked her, "Tell me, is this the price you and Ananias got for the land?" "Yes," she said, "that is the price." Peter said to her, "How could you agree to test the Spirit of the Lord? Look! The feet of the men who buried your husband are at the door, and they will carry you out also." At that moment she fell down at his feet and died. Then the young men came in and, finding her dead, carried her out and buried her beside her husband. Great fear seized the whole church and all who heard about these events. (Acts 5:1-11)

What was going on here? Why were Ananias and Sapphira lying, saying that they were giving the church the full purchase price? There was no established law; they were free to do what they wished with the property and the money. Were they motivated by pride? Fear? Did they come under "peer pressure"? Did they feel they were not going to be accepted if they didn't prove themselves? Did they—like most teenagers and adults—feel pressured to perform? Had they seen the esteem that Barnabas and others had received and become ambitious for it? Were they brought to this point through years of being consumed by what others thought, seeking after the praise of men? Were they legalistic, seeing law where there was no law?

I don't think the text is clear about the motives of Ananias and Sapphira, but I have seen all these responses as we have sought to be a community of people trying to seek the Lord. I have seen them in me, as a leader. I have seen them among my brothers and sisters in our community. And I have seen them in other communities to which we have related.

"UNDERGROUND" LEGALISM

LEGALISM is our effort to find acceptance with God or with others simply on the basis of our conformity to a set of rules, practices, or teachings.

As a community, we were bound by legalism. Through the years we had received much wisdom about living the Christian life in community. We incorporated it into our body of teaching and pattern of life. We learned about daily prayer, meeting in small groups, commitment, accountability, repairing broken relationships, healthy and unhealthy patterns of speech. Each teaching was a gift that helped us to grow and overcome obstacles in our life together in the Lord.

As time went on, we spent a great deal of energy getting all these things to work right. God had given us responsibility to work and build community life, and we needed to be faithful to the things he had given us. So, with the best of motives, we began to rely on the things he gave us rather than the Spirit he gave us. We spent most of our time talking about our life together in Christ rather than about Christ, who is our life. We began to prefer our knowledge—our set way of doing things—over God the giver of knowledge, making the same decision Adam and Eve made in choosing the tree of knowledge of good and evil over the tree of life.

Note that we didn't consider "our way of life" as being a set of established rules. The idea of rules had always had a negative connotation to me—unless I was at a sporting event, teaching in high school (which I did for six years), or relating to my children. Rules were for children. A rule was something you had to follow even if you didn't understand it.

I never thought of our community as having rules. What we had was a way of life, patterns of life, community teachings. As a community, we felt called to family-type relationships as brothers and sisters. Our name, "House of God's Light," was significant, the scriptural word *house* referring to the family (e.g., house of David, household of God). We believed we were called as a family within the church to be a dwelling place for God, through whom his light could shine. We believed that our calling to be a community was a gift, not for us alone, but to be given to others.

If we had no "rules," why do I say that a fundamental problem we had was legalism? For some years we didn't recognize legalism for what it was—a hidden sin that needed to be rooted out. I see three reasons for our legalism being hidden and hard to detect.

1. PEOPLE CAN FLOURISH UNDER LEGALISM

To begin with, many members did flourish in our midst. Actually, most people can benefit by putting some order and discipline in their lives—increasing their prayer time, being accountable for their commitments.

Others, who were struggling under guilt, continued to strive, projecting the appearance of health and success. It was only natural for us to focus on what appeared to be good fruit and to excuse the rest.

As a parent of four children, I can see how my actions affect each of my children differently. Some are profoundly and negatively affected by my weaknesses or sins, while others seem to flourish in the same atmosphere as they respond and compensate. As a result, the child who appears successful justifies my view of myself as a "good parent." Conversely, the one who struggles becomes the problem child—he, not I, having the problem.

This was the case in our community. Our successes justified our less-than-healthy actions. And what about those who didn't thrive in our midst? Well, we could say that *they* were the ones with the problem. (Does this sound at all familiar to you?)

2. LEGALISM ATTRACTS LEGALISTS

THERE'S A SECOND REASON legalism remained hidden. I suspect that people who joined the community were attracted by the desire for righteousness and godly character, having an internal tendency toward legalism. For some, legalism was already a part of their religious milieu. A legalistic approach to Christianity may have been what attracted some to community in the first place.

There are some superficial benefits to legalism. When things are black and white, it's easier, safer, less messy. We can depend on the lines and boxes drawn for us to stay within, rather than on a daily, active relationship with the

Lord. It's easier to serve a cause or obey a law than to pursue a relationship.

Perhaps you too may be a bit like the older brother who took comfort in saying, "Look! All these years I've been slaving for you and never disobeyed your orders" (Luke 15:29). As I see it, the older brother forsook his relationship with his father and sought to gain his place in the family by doing what he was told, by staying within certain safe parameters. He chose the law to be his guardian as a substitute for his father.

3. Something Can Be Better Than Nothing

THE THIRD REASON we didn't see our legalism? Well, standards of behavior, ideals, patterns of life can be a positive, not a negative, factor. Godly standards *do* call us on to holiness and remind us of what we really want to do. They support us and help us to do what is in our heart to do. Though legalism is a trap on the "rigid" side of a scale, Christians primarily concerned with freedom in the Spirit can fall into a trap on the other extreme—casting off restraint and falling into license, like the younger brother in the parable. (As an example, I was once rebuked as a "legalist" for suggesting that people be on time for meetings.) License and lack of concern for others are not the antidote for legalism.

Paul addressed both of these traps in his letter to the Galatian Christians. Some Jewish believers were trying to convince Gentile converts that circumcision and other Old Testament observances (regulations and rules) were requirements for them. Paul wrote, "I am astonished that you are so quickly deserting the one who called you by the grace of

Christ and are turning to a different Gospel—which is really no Gospel at all" (Gal. 1:6). This strict restraint was a direct attack on the "good news." He warned them not to let themselves become "burdened by a yoke of slavery" (Gal. 5:1). Then he went on to warn them not to "use their freedom to indulge the sinful nature; rather, serve one another in love."

Patterns, rules, customs, and practices serve a purpose. They help keep us on a path—rather than getting lost in the woods. Every group has formal, informal, or tacit rules and some way of rewarding those who keep the rules. Anyone who joins a group is off balance for a while until he learns the patterns of the group and how to fit in, if indeed he wants to fit in.

Twenty years ago, a friend of mine joined a religious order, dedicating herself to live and work and pray among the poorest people in the world. We had a chance to visit with her about a year and a half after she joined the order. To our surprise and dismay, she spoke and acted very differently from the woman we had known. I didn't feel I was talking to the same person. She had drawn a new religious identity from the group she was with.

After another year and a half, I saw her again. I saw another change. She acted much the same as she had during the earlier visit, using many of the same phrases and mannerisms, yet this time I enjoyed being with her more, because I encountered the Lord's presence in her life. Her identity was more clearly founded in him, not in her community's patterns.

Fifteen years later we got together again. By this time, most of the distinctive phrases and mannerisms had disappeared. I had a delightful visit. I could experience not only the presence of the Lord, but also the presence of the person I had appreciated before she joined the order.

If you have been following the Lord for more than a few years, you might be able to trace a similar pattern in your own life. At the beginning, you may have adopted speech and behavior patterns that were new to you but characteristic of the church or renewal group you had become part of. There is nothing wrong with all this; it is simply part of our growth process. The real danger is not so much in following religious patterns but in failing to recognize what you are doing and failing to realize that you need to grow out of it. As time goes on, the abiding presence of the Lord should shine forth, enhancing one's own natural personality.

RELIGION: WORTHY OR WORTHLESS?

SOME REFER TO THIS PATTERN as becoming "religious." They might even attribute it to the work of a "religious spirit." For them, the word *religion* is a negative term. But I don't believe the term needs to be negative.

I use the word *religion* in a more positive sense. To me religion is simply the way we live out what we believe. It is the daily things we do to express our faith. It is the actions we take *because of* what we know and believe to be true. *Because* I believe that Jesus Christ is Lord of my life, I spend time with him in prayer every day. *Because* I believe that the Lord has called me to be a Roman Catholic, I go to Mass and confession and raise my children as Catholic Christians. *Because* I believe the Lord has called me to be part of an interdenominational charismatic community, I worship in a particular way, and I am committed to a particular body of people.

In this sense, religion is a good thing that sometimes has a bad reputation—often for some good reasons! The Epistle of James describes a kind of religion that is wonderful to have: "Religion which God our Father accepts as pure and faultless is this: to look after orphans and widows in their distress and to keep oneself from being polluted by the world" (James 1:27). Yet the preceding verse says that if we do not keep a tight rein on our tongue, then we deceive ourselves and "our religion is worthless" (James 1:26).

So religion can be extremely valuable or it can be utterly worthless. Its richness is found in the ways it gives expression to our relationship with God. The concrete, daily practice of Christianity is good, except when it becomes a substitute for a challenging, exciting, and fruitful personal relationship with the living Christ. It is good except when it obscures the need for a daily dependence on the saving power of the risen Lord. Then we find ourselves in the condition Paul warns us about—having a form of godliness but denying its power (2 Tim. 3:5).

The patterns of our Christian life and the wisdom the Lord has given us for our life together in the body of Christ— all the things I am collectively referring to as "religion"—are good. They point the way; they support our faith. *Yet they do not save us.* To fall into a reliance on the things we do— how often or how long we pray, how much we serve, or how "right" our way of doing things is—is to be robbed of the power of our faith, of the dynamic working of the Holy Spirit.

Jesus deals with this issue in an incident recorded in the Gospel of Mark. The Pharisees criticize Jesus for letting his disciples dispense with some of the ritual regulations of cleansing.

So the Pharisees and teachers of the law asked Jesus, "Why don't your disciples live according to the tradition of the elders instead of eating their food with 'unclean' hands?" He replied, "Isaiah was right when he prophesied about you hypocrites; as it is written: 'These people honor me with their lips, but their hearts are far from me. They worship me in vain; their teachings are but rules taught by men.' You have let go of the commands of God and are holding on to the traditions of men. And he said to them: "You have a fine way of setting aside the commands of God in order to observe your own traditions!" (Mark 7:5-9)

FIRST THINGS FIRST

THE DIFFERENCE between the commands of God and the traditions of men is not always clear to us. For example, exactly what does it mean to "keep the Sabbath holy," to "honor your father and your mother"?

Yet the Bible is clear about what our priorities should be. We should not take the things that God puts at the top of the list and place them at the bottom—or any place in between. If we fail to heed God's true priorities, we may become as blind as the Pharisees Jesus rebuked. He told them, "You have a fine way of setting aside the commands of God in order to observe your own traditions!" (Mark 7:9).

On another occasion Jesus made the point clear to "keep first things first":

> *At that time Jesus went through the grainfields on the Sabbath. His disciples were hungry and began to pick some heads of grain and eat them. When the Pharisees saw this, they said to him, "Look! Your disciples are doing what is unlawful on the Sabbath." He answered, "Haven't you read what David did when he and his companions were hungry? He entered the house of God and he and his companions ate the consecrated bread—which was not lawful for them to do, but only for the priests. Or haven't you read in the Law that on the Sabbath the priests in the temple desecrate the day and yet are innocent? I tell you that one greater than the temple is here. If you had known what these words mean, 'I desire mercy, not sacrifice,' you would not have condemned the innocent. For the Son of Man is Lord of the Sabbath."* (Matt. 12:1-8)

Jesus is Lord of the Sabbath. He himself is primary, and everything else is subject to him. Even things that are clearly from God, like the Sabbath, can obscure the One they are meant to reveal—if we fail to keep Jesus primary. The Pharisees, for example, were so focused on the Sabbath that they could not see it was right and good to heal on the Sabbath.

As for our community, we were so focused on our patterns and structures (though we wouldn't call them rules) that we failed to truly see and acknowledge God, the giver of our unity. Because there is value in patterns and structures, we embraced them wholeheartedly, not noticing that we had become enslaved to them.

FEAR PLAYS A ROLE IN LEGALISM

L EGALISM, as we noted earlier, is our effort to find acceptance with God or with others on the basis of our conformity to a set of rules, practices, or teachings.

What can drive our efforts to win the acceptance of others? Fear of what they will think. Fear of their judgment, especially if they are people we see as authority figures. Isn't that what drove my compulsion to wear tight pants? Mightn't that have been what prompted Ananias and Sapphira to lie to the church leaders? They wanted to look generous, even if they weren't. Isn't that what often determines our commitments? Is how much I pray, fast, serve, or study determined by what others are doing? (I want to do enough so that no one will criticize me, but not more than I have to.)

Fear can drive us to feel "safe" only when we feel we have all the right answers, *right now.*

Several years ago, some members of our community attended a conference where a well-known and highly respected preacher spoke very authoritatively about right and wrong ways to resist the devil through prayer. His teaching in this area did not mesh with our community's experience. In fact, there was total disagreement between the two. Some in our group responded by accepting what he said as the final word on the subject.

Of course, it is good to repent quickly and make corrections when we realize we are moving in the wrong way. But it is wrong to repent and change our course without understanding and conviction. I was certainly challenged by the speaker's statements. I listened. I knew there was something right about what he said. But I was also uncomfortable with some of it. I had a contradictory testimony based on something I believed the Lord had given us.

I realized that I shouldn't move quickly to change my position—when that move would have been motivated merely by peer pressure or, rather, authority pressure (fear). I had learned that the fear of man can cause us to give up our conviction too quickly, without sorting out what is from the Lord and what is not. We should always seek to understand the truth behind what we are doing, so that our hearts can remain set on the heavenly goals, not on the earthly practices.

God can and does often speak to us through others. Yet the Lord will not excuse us from personal responsibility because of what someone else has told us. Nor does he want us to refrain from speaking his truth in love for fear that we will offend someone. The fear of man can rob the people of God of the prophetic voice. Lamentations says, "The visions of your prophets were false and worthless; they did not expose your sin to ward off your captivity. The oracles they gave you were false and misleading" (2:14). Various movements within the church are meant to serve prophetically. If the fear of offending or being misunderstood—or the fear of conflict—takes precedence over serving the Lord, the work of the Holy Spirit can be compromised.

In his first letter to the Corinthians, Paul tells them he is sending Timothy and notes: "He will remind you of my way of life in Christ Jesus, which agrees with what I teach" (4:17). In the letter, Paul corrects the church for divisions, immorality, disorder, false teaching, and other abuses. Here he sends his "son" Timothy as an example, to remind the church how to live in relationship to sound teaching.

Proverbs 29:25 says, "Fear of man will prove to be a snare, but whoever trusts in the Lord is kept safe." Again, the trap is in extreme reactions to conformity and authority. It is right to esteem and listen to our teachers. It is good to honor and respect our leaders. It is even good to do all things in a "fitting and orderly way" (1 Cor. 14:40). But God, not man, is the focus and authority of our lives.

One day as I was sharing some of these thoughts with the community, one young man acknowledged that, while trying to make a certain decision, he had been most concerned about what *I* would think. He said he could picture a little Neal Lozano sitting on his shoulder. At that moment, his fear of my opinion was superseding the centrality of Christ in his life.

RELEASE FROM LEGALISM AND FEAR

THIS YOUNG MAN needed to understand the truth that David expressed: "My eyes are ever on the Lord, for only he will release my feet from the snare" (Ps. 25:15). Only the Lord will release us from the snares of legalism and fear of man.

Apart from the love and acceptance available in Christ, we spend our lives trying to figure out the rules, trying to adjust our behavior to the expert of the hour, trying to measure up, hoping we will overcome the emptiness and insecurity within. We end up with a pair of pants that doesn't quite fit, a pair that we will soon outgrow and discard—only to search for another pair that will fit us better.

Paul asked the Galatians these questions: *Did you receive the Spirit by observing the Law or by believing what you heard? Are you so foolish? After beginning in the Spirit, are you now trying to attain your goal by human effort?* (Gal. 3:2-3).

When our community woke up to our problem with legalism and fear, we had to answer "Yes" to these questions. Yes, we were that foolish. Yes, we had fallen into the trap of seeking to attain our goal by human effort, forgetting that the Spirit is given freely to those who believe.

Change for us began with a revisiting of the Spirit of God. He came and filled a void that had grown within us. We saw that patterns or standards cease being instruments of grace when they become the basis for gaining acceptance with God or with one another.

Getting free of the impact of legalism meant laying aside many of the "gifts" we had received. Just as Abraham placed Isaac on the altar, we placed our community, its name, its teachings, and our patterns of meeting on the altar.

We decided we would seek a fresh revelation of the person of Jesus Christ and his kingdom—and that we would not take anything off the altar that he did not in some way give back with new perspective and light.

We continued to meet, but we refused to hold on to our meetings, or any other pattern of our life, as though we couldn't be a community without it. We decided that we would teach about community no more than once a month, reserving the other meetings to proclaim the person of Christ and the Good News of the kingdom. We changed how members could be related to the community so that whether or not they chose to be fully involved in community life, they could still be fully recognized as our brothers and sisters, just as it is in a typical family, where members don't always live in the same house or work together but always remain family. This removed much of the unnecessary pressure to conform.

I share these changes not necessarily to suggest a course of action for other groups, but to indicate what was necessary for us as we faced the impact which legalism and the pressure to conform had made on us.

Years have passed. And some things we laid on the altar we still long to take up again. Sometimes it is difficult to discern when you are being faithful to what God has called you to do and when you are being irresponsible. Is it wisdom we are operating under? Or is it the effects of having been burned out by our own human effort? Sometimes I question, "Lord, how long until we can return to deeper community life? Will we ever make it through this time of transition?"

Then I recall the level of love for God that is present in our midst and the quality of our relationships that have grown through the testing of the years and the zeal that is ours to serve the Lord. No law can impart life. Perfect love casts out fear. Community life is not a matter of talk but of power. It is not a matter of order but of relationships joined together in Christ. "Rules," like pants, are necessary, but the best rules are the ones that are transcended by our love for Christ.

For in Christ Jesus neither circumcision nor uncircumcision has any value. The only thing that counts is faith expressing itself in love. (Gal. 5:6)

For God did not give us a spirit of timidity, but a spirit of power, love and self-discipline. (2 Tim.1:7)

4

Weakness and Strength

DID WE IN OUR OWN STRENGTH CONFIDE,
OUR STRIVING WOULD BE LOSING.

— Martin Luther

THE IDOL OF COMMUNITY

A DECADE AGO, if someone had said to me that our community was not properly focused on the Lord, I would never have accepted it. But as our community began dealing with religious pride, an undeniable truth emerged: we were relying more on one another and on the community than on the Lord. We had virtually made an idol out of community. We prided ourselves in the strength of our own unity. And we were spending more time talking about our life together than on proclaiming the saving power of the Gospel.

The secondary things in our life—which were good things—had come to look very much like the primary things. As a result, we were losing the grace-filled life in the Holy Spirit.

CRUSHING PRIDE

R ELIGIOUS PRIDE takes what is secondary and makes it primary. It focuses on our own perceived strengths, not on our utter dependence on God.

I started to learn something about this in 1985, at a Vineyard Ministries "Signs and Wonders" conference in California. It was led by John Wimber, a Christian leader whose ministry has invigorated believers throughout the world. Vineyard conferences are noted for helping Christians open their hearts and minds to the working of God's supernatural power, both in their own lives and in works of ministry. In that milieu, the power of the kingdom, the manifest reign of God, crushed my pride, exposed my sin, and brought me into the embracing arms of Jesus.

I could hardly believe what I was seeing: God was using young, seemingly immature people to pray for and heal the sick. In my estimation, they did not dress properly or act right; yet God was using them powerfully.

In this conference, I also learned something about honesty. John Wimber described himself as "a fat man trying to get to heaven," as "loose change in God's pocket, to be spent any way God wants." This godly man could acknowledge that he was still the prodigal come home, unworthy to be called a son. Though he acknowledged his unworthiness, he manifested the generous love of the Father, seeking to give away what God had given him.

Over the previous two years I had suffered from a serious back problem. Quite often, right before a significant spiritual event, I would find myself in bed for a week, unable to move. True to form, a week before my scheduled trip to the conference in Anaheim, I ended up in bed again, not knowing if I would be able to make the trip. The day I left I couldn't lift my bag or sit for more than a few minutes at a time. As is my custom, I had gotten the lowest priced airline ticket, which, in this case, involved three changeovers—requiring me to endure the painful ordeal of sitting through three takeoffs and landings. The rest of the time I spent standing in the back of the plane convincing the flight attendants not to send me to my seat when the seat belt sign went on.

As I walked into the first session of the conference, I felt that at any moment my back spasm would return and I would be forced to spend the week confined to my motel room. For much of the conference, I found myself standing or lying down on the floor in the back of the room.

My physical weakness revealed my spiritual condition. I had done my best, tried my hardest to serve the Lord, and had come to the end. I had nothing more to give. Spiritually I had come to a place of weakness and brokenness. Having a skewed view of strength and weakness, I had been unable to accept and yield to my condition. But in the presence of this man's honest awareness of his weakness, I too was able to be weak. I was able to acknowledge my utter dependence on God—and he took hold of my life all over again.

While singing Vineyard "love songs" to God, my heart began to break. I wept before the Lord. I was falling in love all over again. My return was based not on my strength, but on his amazing love and compassion—which evoked a deepening recognition of my unworthiness. Only in returning to my first love did I know how cold my heart had grown. At the conference I was taught and empowered to pray for the sick, and I saw that praying for the sick is an expression of our utter weakness, inability, and dependence on God. It is a means by which we can be a channel to others of the compassion which God has revealed to us.

At this conference, I—the older brother who had never realized how far from the Father he really was—became like the younger brother. I was welcomed home, accepted, restored, and forgiven. I found the pearl of great price again. To this day, I am grateful that when I returned, my brothers and sisters accepted the new me and, together, we began to seek first the kingdom of God, trusting that all things would be given.

We began a process of rediscovering how much God wanted to fulfill his call to make us a community by his grace—as we sought first his kingdom, not our "common life" of which we were so proud.

IN WHAT DO WE BOAST?

THROUGHOUT MY CHRISTIAN LIFE I had worked hard to distance myself from any form of weakness. Especially as I came to be perceived as a Christian leader, I saw my success and my victory over personal problems as a testimony that would help others to believe. Weakness was not a source of blessing; it was an enemy.

I remember reacting negatively when people would say, "People just need Jesus as a crutch in life." For years I would disagree, using this logic: "It's not that we are so needy or weak, it's simply that Jesus is the fullness of truth and life."

While my response was true to a point, I missed the
opportunity to boast of the things that demonstrated my
weakness and Christ's strength. I could have said, "I need
Jesus *more* than a cripple needs a crutch. I need him for my
daily existence. I need him more than I need food."

But I had fallen into the trap. I thought I wanted to be a
strong Christian, but what I *really* wanted was to be a strong
person, to be strong enough not to need Jesus anymore—in
the same subtle way the House of God's Light Community
wanted to be strong enough to boast of its own unity; in the
same subtle way that churches boast of their programs and
facilities and outreach ministries.

Who wants to boast of his weaknesses rather than
strengths? After all, we live in a society that values strength
and hides from weakness. We run and hide from those
things that reveal our weakness. We hide from the elderly
and the handicapped, we abort our children, we adjust our
appearances through surgery, we flee from the poor and the
odoriferous.

We simply don't want to face being vulnerable. If you're
married, you've probably learned some invaluable lessons
about vulnerability and weakness. At times, I've felt that my
wife needed me always to be strong. But what I have inad-
vertently communicated by this approach is, "I don't need
you."

The fact is, I do need her. And if I don't reveal my need
to my wife, she won't know how important her life and presence are to me. By choosing her as a partner for life, I have
chosen to become vulnerable.

Being weak means being honest with ourselves. That's not what we by nature want to do. We want to deny our weakness, rationalize it, or call it something else. Scripture warns us to be careful if we think we are strong, lest we fall. Understanding our weakness is vital to our grasping the message of the Gospel.

The apostle Paul faced a particular challenge in the Corinthian church. In his second letter to them, he was responding to false teachers who were commending themselves. Paul wrote, "Such men are false apostles, deceitful workmen, masquerading as apostles of Christ" (11:13). He saw them as aggressive, manipulative and controlling (11:20), and he was driven to a godly jealousy and concern for the church:

> *I am jealous for you with a godly jealousy. I promised you to one husband, to Christ, so that I might present you as a pure virgin to him. But I am afraid that just as Eve was deceived by the serpent's cunning, your minds may somehow be led astray from your sincere and pure devotion to Christ.* (2 Cor. 11:2-3)

How was he to protect the Corinthian believers from being led astray? Boasting was out. He was on record:

> *May I never boast except in the cross of our Lord Jesus Christ, through which the world has been crucified to me, and I to the world.* (Gal. 6:14)

> *For I resolved to know nothing while I was with you except Jesus Christ and him crucified. I came*

to you in weakness and fear, and with much trem-
bling. (1 Cor. 2:2-3).

But, "Let him who boasts boast in the Lord" (2 Cor.
10:17).

Nevertheless, in order to protect them, Paul decided to
boast. What did he boast of? Spiritual gifts? Healings?
Church growth? Abilities? Awards? College degrees? No! He
boasted of hardships, persecutions, suffering, the burden of
concern he carried for all the churches, and an experience of
God that was beyond his ability to communicate. All these
things were the opposite of worldly success and power. They
produced dependence on God. They were things he could do
only by grace. His weakness was the means of God's grace
being active in his life.

He said, "If I must boast, I will boast of the things that
show my weakness" (2 Cor. 11:30). Paul was being consis-
tent, after all. To boast of one's weakness is to boast in the
Lord, the Crucified One, because it is our very weakness that
reveals the power of the cross of Christ to others.

Paul was used in mighty ways to heal, to deliver, to set the
captives free, and he was given great revelations from God.
Yet his boast was in something that afflicted him:

To keep me from becoming conceited because of these
surpassingly great revelations, there was given me a
thorn in my flesh, a messenger of Satan, to torment
me. Three times I pleaded with the Lord to take it
away from me. But he said to me, "My grace is

sufficient for you, for my power is made perfect in weakness." Therefore I will boast all the more gladly about my weaknesses, so that Christ's power may rest on me. That is why, for Christ's sake, I delight in weaknesses, in insults, in hardships, in persecutions, in difficulties. For when I am weak, then I am strong. (2 Cor. 12:7-10)

Through his suffering, Paul understood the great paradox that when we are weak, we are strong. Because God's power is made perfect in weakness, our weakness is something to take great delight in.

We confuse the strength that we are to have in the Lord with the strength we have in the flesh. We often disdain the very weakness that God has permitted in our lives to produce godly character and strength. When we read about Paul boasting of his weakness and declaring that when he is weak he is strong, we put qualifications on it. We put distance between ourselves and his experience. We don't understand, and we find it threatening to even try.

Being weak means recognizing and accepting thorns in the flesh. What are the thorns in your life? Is there someone with whom you are having a difficulty: your child, your parent, your spouse, a co-worker? Is there someone who brings out the worst in you, someone who makes you look bad, someone who opposes you in everything you try to do? Do you have a physical problem? These things often serve God's purposes; they are the things that keep us humble and under God's grace.

THE STRENGTH OF THE WEAK

W HEN I SPEAK OF WEAKNESS, I am not referring to sin but to our vulnerability to sin and our utter dependence on God. Webster defines weakness as lacking strength; being frail or feeble; lacking moral strength or willpower. Paul defines it in terms of insults, hardships, and difficulties.

Understanding our weakness is vital to our grasping the message of the Gospel. Jesus said we must remain in him, for apart from him we can do nothing.

King David describes weakness in poetic terms, crying out to God, his strength:

> *I love you, O LORD, my strength. The LORD is my rock, my fortress and my deliverer; my God is my rock, in whom I take refuge. He is my shield and the horn of my salvation, my stronghold. I call to the LORD, who is worthy of praise, and I am saved from my enemies. The cords of death entangled me; the torrents of destruction overwhelmed me. The cords of the grave coiled around me; the snares of death confronted me. In my distress I called to the LORD; I cried to my God for help. From his temple he heard my voice; my cry came before him, into his ears.* (Ps. 18:1-6)

Beginning with a declaration of who God is, David openly and honestly confesses the truth of his situation and, in his distress, he cries out to God for help.

Throughout his life David understood the truth about weakness. When he went out to face Goliath, Saul offered him the king's armor. No. He chose five stones instead. He chose weak things of the world and defeated Goliath by the power of God, so that "the whole world will know that there is a God in Israel" (1 Sam. 17:46). Like David, Jesus himself cried out in human weakness.

During the days of Jesus' life on earth, he offered up prayers and petitions with loud cries and tears to the one who could save him from death, and he was heard because of his reverent submission. (Heb. 5:7)

When he offered up these prayers with loud cries and tears, it's likely that others heard Jesus. If so, he imparted something of great value to his disciples in his cries; he taught them that strength is found in weakness.

Jesus, like David, chose weakness to defeat Satan. Instead of five stones, Jesus chose five wounds to defeat the enemy. We too defeat the enemy, not by man's armor, but by what God works into us through the weakness we embrace. Our real strength is that we are trusting in the Lord and looking to God for what we need.

WEAKNESS AS A GOOD TEACHER

THERE'S TRUTH in the assertion that true healers—and leaders—are wounded ones. It is out of our brokenness that we reveal the power and love of God to others. We cannot give what we have not received. As we give leadership and counsel, we can lead the way in being honest about our struggles. If we present ourselves as more holy than we are, then those who hear us and know us will tend to either present themselves as better than they are, or become discouraged by their own weakness.

Let our leadership challenge others to be honest and sincere in their struggles rather than successful in appearance. Let us reveal our need as we serve others, so that they may know that every member of the body of Christ is important and needed by the others.

There is faulty thinking in the idea that if we appear to be perfect, we will be great testimonies to other people, especially our children. If we *don't* reveal our weakness to our children, they can get discouraged and lose hope that they will ever be able to be godly men and women. If we appear to be perfect, they will think that they need to be perfect, too. Children need to know that we parents need their prayers. We should be honest in difficult times (while being careful to be the parent and not reverse the roles). They need to see how we go through a problem, not just the results of the resolution.

This lesson was powerfully demonstrated in the life of one New England pastor, Lionel (Lee) Whiston, a popular author, retreat leader, and conference speaker. The classic story of how the Whiston family grew closer together through Lee's "peanut brittle weakness" is a memorable illustration which warrants our attention.†

---

† I am grateful to the Whiston family, especially Ruth Whiston Upshall (who played a key role in the story), for their enthusiastic permission to include "The Peanut Brittle Story" here. The story was first published nearly thirty years ago as "When Weakness Makes Men Strong" in *Are You Fun to Live With?* by Lionel A. Whiston (Canton, Ohio: Life Enrichment Publishers, 1968). The book is now out of print.

THE PEANUT BRITTLE STORY

L EE WHISTON knelt at the altar rail in his church. He prayed silently, asking how he could dedicate his life more truly to God.

"God, will you make me the person I ought to be? Will you make me the father, the husband, the man that you really want me to be? Come inside, into my thoughts, my emotions, every part of me."

He was really offering himself to God, as completely as he knew how. And the thought flashed through his mind, "What about the peanut brittle?"

Shocked by the incongruity of the notion, Lee said, "Be serious, God! I'm asking how I can dedicate myself more completely to you. What's a little candy?"

But God knew what he was saying to Lee Whiston.

It was a custom in the Whiston family for one of the children to go to the candy store on Friday evening to buy a bag of peanut brittle or gum drops as a weekend treat. Lee and his wife Irma liked candy as much as their three children did, but, not wanting to "overdo a good thing," they had established this custom of a modest Saturday splurge.

The candy was for everyone; it was ceremoniously placed in a dish and passed from one member of the family to another. It was understood that no one was to take the candy alone. In fact, the children often heard their father say, "If you take a piece 'on the sly,' no candy for a month."

But Lee had fallen into the habit of regarding himself as "above the law" where the candy was concerned. After the children were in bed on Friday night he'd often find his way to the pantry and satisfy his sweet tooth with a piece or two of "forbidden fruit." To be sure, he knew he wasn't playing fair with the family, but he would pacify his conscience with such rationalizations as, "Well, who paid for it?" or "Who made the rule?" or "Nobody needs that bit of extra energy more than I do."

When Lee got up from the altar rail he tried to think about something else, but the peanut brittle stuck to his mind as it had so often stuck to his teeth. By the time he got home from church he knew he would have to confess to his cheating, and he determined to do so right after dinner.

Surprising, how difficult it was for Lee to admit his crime to his teen-age sons and ten-year-old daughter! Still, as he stumbled through an awkward confession, he comforted himself with the thought that one of them would come to his rescue with, "That's okay, Dad. You work hard and you have a right to favors like that."

But no one spoke up.

In the silence, Lee felt like a condemned prisoner waiting for the judge to pronounce sentence. Nothing much was said. When the children had gone out and Lee's wife was in the kitchen, washing dishes, Lee thought to himself, *That's the end of that.*

But it wasn't.

A few days later Lee and his wife were taking advantage of the late-evening quiet to catch up on some reading. The quiet was suddenly interrupted by sobs coming from a bedroom.

"That's Ruth," Irma said.

Going to her young daughter's room, Irma found Ruth with her head buried in a pillow, trying to stifle her sobs. She picked her up, brought her into the living room and put her on Lee's lap. The tears were flowing and her cheeks were swollen.

"Ruthie, what's the matter?" Lee asked.

"I'm the thief," she sniffled.

"What thief?" he said in astonishment. "What did you take?"

"The cake."

Lee's wife raised her eyebrows and shook her head in bewilderment. Lee pursued the matter. "What cake are you talking about?"

"The chocolate cake!" More tears.

The *chocolate* cake! Suddenly, everything made sense.

Seven months earlier, on a Saturday morning, Lee's wife had baked a three-layer chocolate cake, iced it, and put it on a plate in the refrigerator. That evening when she began to prepare dinner, she found that the cake was missing. So was the plate. They had completely disappeared.

"Don't look at me, Mom," said 16-year-old Lionel. "I didn't even know you made the cake.'

His brother Bill's denial of guilt was equally vehement. "Sure, I thought of taking a piece, but I just took some of the frosting, that's all. I thought you were taking it to a church supper, or something."

Little Ruth's plea of innocence was most persuasive of all. "Mama, I know you're trying to teach us to be good like Jesus, so I didn't touch it."

The parents concluded that it was another piece of mischief on the part of Junior Markham, the "pest" who lived across the street. He had taken different things from the lawn, and the Whistons had once actually caught him in the act. But it had certainly come to a new low when he would come right into the house and open the refrigerator! Oh, would they give him a dirty look the next time they saw him! And, of course, they were proud of their "three little angels."

Now, seven months later, here was little Ruth sobbing out her story.

"Ruthie, what happened?" Lee asked, mystified.

"I wanted to give a party for my friends," she sobbed, "so I took the cake and a bottle of ginger ale out of the refrigerator. We ate all we could. I put the leftovers under my bed and I ate a little bit each night till it was all gone. Then I broke the plate so I wouldn't get found out."

Fresh tears flowed and Ruth said brokenheartedly, "I haven't been able to say my prayers. I wanted all the time to tell you, but I was afraid if I did you wouldn't love me any more. I decided that if I waited until I was twenty-one and then told you, we'd all laugh about it together."

Looking at his daughter, Lee realized how much they were alike. He, too, found it difficult and costly to be honest, especially with his wife. He, too, had been afraid he might not be loved if people knew his faults and the mistakes he had made.

Lee kissed Ruth's swollen eyelids, and new love for her welled up in his heart. "I stole things when I was your age, too," he told her. "Sometimes I even took money from my mother's handbag."

"Even now," he went on, "I have trouble being honest. Remember the peanut brittle?"

"Uh huh," she said tremulously. "When you told us about that I knew I would have to tell you about the cake."

No longer were Lee and Ruth separated by age and status. They were together, not as a righteous father and a naughty little girl, but as two sinners, two thieves. And by mutual confession and God's forgiveness, they had passed from the fellowship of sinners to the fellowship of saints. As he put his arm around her, Christ was there between two thieves—just as on Calvary two thousands years ago.

In Weakness . . .

As long as Lee had been leading from strength, pulling rank as a father who was always right, who always knew the answers, there was distance. "I wanted to tell you about it but I was afraid you wouldn't love me."

When he came, not in his righteousness and in his strength, but in his weakness, Lee was able to lay down a bridge which Ruth could walk over. "He'll understand now. He's a thief too. He stole. He knows all about it. Maybe he'll understand why I stole."

"As a parent," recalled Lee, "I had been fond of pulling rank, and I had more than once told my children about my boyhood activities, never telling them the bad things I did, only the good things. My wife, too, had a habit of pulling out a report card that was generally straight A's and showing the children. We were leading from strength, pulling rank on them—as if we, as their parents, were doing much better than they were."

"But," noted Lee, "when I was willing to become the liar that I was, the thief that I was, and be honest and lead from my weakness, I was able to hug a little child who had been a stranger in her heart for seven months. We came together in a way that was never before possible. The encounter had served to reach an unresolved area in Ruth's life, as I unwittingly spoke Ruth's language."

It required Lee to forego his prerogatives as a parent and jeopardize his status in the eyes of his children. His pride was humbled; he climbed down from his pedestal. He didn't "lead from strength," seeking to be perfect and righteous in the family's sight. He "led from weakness," becoming a fellow sinner with his wife and children.

This costly act of self-disclosure placed him in a vulnerable position where his daughter could accept or reject him as she chose. She might have thought: *My father is a thief; therefore it is all right for me to steal.* Parental respect might have vanished.

Instead, she chose to "walk over the bridge" he had laid down. She entered into his heart and experience, and he into hers. Both of them felt a nearness to each other and a nearness to God.

The next day Ruth courageously told her story to her brothers and this prompted similar confessions on their part. One of the boys owned up to cutting corners on his piano practice; the other admitted that he had falsely claimed to have finished his homework on more than one occasion. The entire experience resulted in the creation of a new, stronger bond in the Whiston home, as each person realized he was part of a family of forgiven sinners.

CLOSE TO HOME

OFTEN ENOUGH, God provides us with invaluable lessons about weakness and strength very "close to home."

For quite a few years, I prided myself in my ability to sit down with folks and help them resolve their relational difficulties. That is, until I met my match—my own children. All too often, I failed in my efforts to help resolve their conflicts and restore relationships.

One day as I was headed upstairs to help resolve a conflict (one more time), I asked God for help. Immediately a story came to mind about the pastor of a large church. Whenever there were problems among the leaders, he would gather them all together and begin to pray and confess his sins. As he prayed, the others would be led into repentance and humility before the Lord, and reconciliation would follow.

Since I had nothing left to give my children, I thought I would try it, in desperation, with my sons. Once upstairs, I asked them to kneel with me.

As they knelt by my side, I cried out to God from my heart. Within moments, both of my sons began to weep as they asked God to forgive them and help them. Grace was released and, for several weeks following, there was a work of grace in their hearts, expressed through patience, forbearance, and love.

The normal conflicts eventually returned, but from that point on, there was a new freedom for them to grow through their difficulties. A root of bitterness had been broken, not by human wisdom, but by the power of God manifested through human weakness.

Note Paul's words to the Christians at Corinth: "My message and my preaching were not with wise and persuasive words, but with a demonstration of the Spirit's power, so that your faith might not rest on men's wisdom, but on God's power" (1 Cor. 2:4-5). Paul came to Corinth in weakness, so that their faith might rest in the power of God.

BLESSED ARE THE WEAK

JESUS HIMSELF taught us the principle of weakness and strength. In Matthew, chapter 5, Jesus describes the blessed ones: those who are poor in spirit (who know their need), the meek (who know the greatness of God and therefore their lowliness), the ones that mourn (who feel the pain of loss), the peacemakers (who, like Jesus, suffer the loss of their life for the sake of bringing reconciliation to others), and those who are persecuted for the sake of the Gospel (who have lost or given up their rights).

The attitudes to which Jesus calls us are those of humility, lowliness, and weakness. These are not attitudes we can achieve by willpower or effort. They are developed as we yield to God in the circumstances of our life. He calls us to embrace our weakness, not seeking to be happy on the basis of our own achievement, but rather, trusting in him for happiness that comes from our relationship with him. It is a relationship that increases as we decrease, that is strengthened as we are weakened.

Scripture is clear that our true strength rests in God: "The Lord is my strength and my song" (Ex. 15:2); "The joy of the Lord is your strength" (Neh. 8:10); "Apart from me you can do nothing" (John 15:5).

How do we lose that strength—his strength in our weakness? Judges 16:17 indicates that we lose our strength through sin, and Mark 9:18 shows us that we lose it through unbelief. Sin and unbelief cut us off from the Lord, who is our strength. We are strong only when we are weak enough to confess our sins and trust in his saving power.

CHANGE BEGINS WITH HONESTY

M ANY YEARS AGO our community received some helpful teaching on Christian manhood and manly character. But in our response to the teaching many of us started to grow afraid of our weakness. We became more concerned with what others thought about us and whether or not they knew how insecure we were about our own identity. We wanted to measure up, to be better than we were.

We began to try to change from the outside in, not motivated by love for God, but by a love for ourselves and a denial of our true condition. The Spirit had to teach us again that change takes place not with denial but with honesty.

When we become aware that our lives are not manifesting godly character, we need to admit it and seek to understand it as fully as we can. We need to confess our shortcomings and cry out to God from our weakness. Only then can we act on what we have learned with the confidence that it is God who is producing change in us.

There wasn't anything wrong with the teaching on Christian manhood; what was wrong was our response to it. If we seek to respond to a teaching about Christian life without confessing our weakness, then we will be seeking to grow by our own wisdom and strength apart from the grace of God. To do so is to miss the mark.

Millions of people in twelve-step programs begin their journey by admitting that they are failures, that they are powerless before their addiction. This is a truth not reserved for the addict; it is a truth the Gospel has always proclaimed for all of us. The cross of Christ tells us that we are failures, hopelessly lost. In fact, that is the very reason for the cross. The message of the cross is that we are guilty and condemned, in need of a Savior. The cross declares to us that we are hopelessly weak, that all the wisdom of man is foolishness if it does not come under the cross, which is the wisdom of God.

THE VIEW FROM THE CROSS

SALVATION is an ongoing process. As we experience life's circumstances, the Scriptures, the work of the Holy Spirit, and the teachings of the Church, we are led to a deeper discovery of our blindness, sin, and separation. This gives us a greater awareness of our helplessness, desperation, and dependency on God, which, in turn, leads us to confession of sin and crying out to God. The clarity we have about our need relates directly to the quality of our repentance. We can then earnestly pray with the psalmist: "Out of the depths I cry to you, O Lord" (Ps. 130:1); "I sought the Lord, and he answered me; he delivered me from all my fears" (Ps. 34:4).

We cry out to God in our weakness, and God hears our cries and delivers us. Is deliverance possible apart from weakness? Is salvation possible apart from the cross? Is not God's foolishness greater than the wisdom of man? Should we not then learn to delight in our weakness?

After he was transfigured before them, Jesus told his disciples, "Don't tell anyone what you have seen, until the Son of Man has been raised from the dead" (Matt. 17:9). There are certain things that can never be understood except with a view from the cross, enlightened by the resurrection.

> *Jews demand miraculous signs and Greeks look for wisdom, but we preach Christ crucified: a stumbling block to Jews and foolishness to Gentiles, but to those whom God has called, both Jews and Greeks, Christ the power of God and the wisdom of God. For the foolishness of God is wiser than man's wisdom, and the weakness of God is stronger than man's strength.* (1 Cor. 1:22-25)

The cross is the very foolishness of God; it is the weakness of God. At the cross we see the great paradox. There the Author of Life dies. The One who knows no sin is punished for sin by his loving Father. The cross, which is the wisdom of God, is foolishness to men. The strength of God himself is presented through weakness.

On the cross Jesus bore our weaknesses. He took them on so that we could walk, not in accordance with our weakness, but in accordance with his strength. In Christ we walk in great power and victory. We delight in our weakness because God chose us, "the weak things of the world," to "shame the strong" (1 Cor. 1:27).

Because of his work on the cross, we can—and should—boast in our weakness. Why? Because being weak means being strong. To boast of our weakness enables us to boast of the cross of Christ, "through which the world has been crucified to me, and I to the world" (Gal. 6:14). In Christ we are not lost, but found. In him we are not failures, we walk in victory. We are no longer guilty, but forgiven. In him we are not condemned, but accepted. We no longer need to demonstrate our value by what good we do; we have become good by receiving the life of the Son of God, through the presence of the Holy Spirit.

A WORD ABOUT UNITY

I STARTED this chapter talking about our community having taken pride in the seeming strength of our unity. But now, more than a decade after my 1985 awakening at the Signs and Wonders conference, I can say that being weak has strengthened our unity. Our unity is most real to us when we stand together at the foot of the cross of Christ, standing in need of prayer and grace, and the merciful love of the welcoming Father.

5

Judgment or Mercy

WHEN THIS SON OF YOURS WHO HAS SQUAN-
DERED YOUR PROPERTY WITH PROSTITUTES COMES
HOME . . .

— The older brother

STAN THE MAN

SEVERAL YEARS AGO I was at a leaders' conference with
four other members of our community. It was a wonderful conference, but when it was over, I felt something spiritually lacking in the experience. I soon would know the final
lesson of the trip.

On the morning after the final conference session, we
were up quite early. Our airport ride was scheduled to arrive
at seven o'clock, in plenty of time to make our ten o'clock
flight. When our driver, a member of a sister community,
didn't arrive on time, we waited patiently, cheerfully saying
good-bye to other conference participants on their way to

breakfast. But as time passed, we grew hungry and increasingly anxious about our Sunday afternoon commitments. Our patience thinned, then disappeared. *These conferences were always so well-organized. Things like this were not supposed to happen! What could have gone wrong?*

It was after nine when our ride finally arrived. Believe me, we were standing at the door, ready to throw our bags into the car. Upon greeting the brother (I'll call him Stan), we expected an apologetic "Please forgive me. I was held up because . . . , but now we're on our way."

No. First Stan had to rearrange the junk in his car so that we could get in. When we were finally settled in our seats, there was a moment of uncomfortable silence.

"Just a minute. I'll be right back," he said. He left our company—to go to the restroom!

A few minutes later, we were on the road at last. But I couldn't believe what I heard next.

"I'm not sure how to get out of this town. And, by the way, we're going to have to stop for gas. If we don't, we won't make it to the airport."

That settled it. We were going to miss our plane.

I fought an internal battle. How do I respond to this brother? How do I defuse my frustration, even anger, and the tense atmosphere in the car? My wife and I were sitting in the front seat, and I could feel the "heat" rising from the back seat.

Then driver Stan turned to us and said, "Have you ever heard of John Wimber?"

Oh, no, I thought, but I actually said something like, "Yeah, we've heard of John Wimber."

"Well, on my way over here, I was praying for you, and I had a pain in my wrist and a pain in my head, like somebody was having a migraine headache. I think God wants me to pray for you if you have these symptoms."

During the two weeks before the conference, my wife Janet had been having migraines. But I knew nobody had a wrist problem, and I was silently rejoicing. After all, anybody can have a "word of knowledge" about a headache.

Well, as it turned out, one of the women in the back seat had been having a wrist problem all week long. So we began to pray.

As one thing led to another, the wrist problem was healed. And my wife experienced a powerful manifestation of God's presence—on the way to the airport!

Fortunately we missed our plane, and Stan came into the terminal with us. As he placed his hands on Janet's shoulder to pray for her, she was overcome with a sense of the presence of God. She slumped down in her chair, completely at rest. There we were—with all these airline passengers walking by, staring at Janet sprawled in the chair, several stopping to ask if she needed help.

If you knew my wife, you'd know that she is normally very careful about her demeanor. She's not in the habit of making a spectacle of herself in airport waiting rooms. But when you've waited a long time for such a blessing, you don't really care when God chooses to show up!

Soon enough, we were able to get another plane, and we arrived at our afternoon community meeting just in time. During the meeting, one of the back-seat passengers in Stan's car shared his own story of the trip. All the way to the airport, he had harbored judgment toward Stan. Even when the power of God was evident, he had struggled with the fact that God had used this brother who had never even apologized for being late and inconveniencing us. He had expected a more proper response from someone so late, someone who was a part of a disciplined community like ours.

In our meeting, our brother confessed his anger about the situation—and his disbelief. As he shared his judgments, several women in the community began weeping. He was expressing the same kind of judgmental attitude and intolerance that they had experienced within our community. Now it was exposed to the light. I sensed the Lord saying, "Now it's time"—time to deal with the hidden sin of judgment.

Over the years, the Lord had repeatedly spoken to us about judgment: "Don't judge one another. ... You're judging. ... Repent. ..." And we had always said, "O yes, Lord, we repent." But we had no idea what we were repenting of. We had no idea how to deal with judgment. Through Stan, God's grace was released to us, and the Lord revealed new insights into the hidden sin of judgment.

(As I reflect now on that eventful weekend, I wonder if "Stan" really exists or if God sent an angel to pick us up that day.)

SUBSEQUENT LESSONS

OUR EXPERIENCE WITH STAN led our community to a wonderful time of healing and growth. We began to be convicted of our judgments and convinced that we should turn to mercy. Our discovering process started with the grave warning found in James 2:13: "Judgment without mercy will be shown to anyone who has not been merciful." The verse continues, "Mercy triumphs over judgment." Through mercy, we have great victory, great power, and great hope in the face of the judgments we make and those made against us. Judgment brings more judgment and mercy brings more mercy. Jesus says, "Do not judge, or you too will be judged" and "Blessed are the merciful for they will be shown mercy" (Matt. 7:1; 5:7). Knowing that mercy breeds mercy and judgment breeds judgment has a profound effect on the way we live.

We had a difficult time understanding judgment and how to turn from it—such a buried, internal sin. Our judgments generally simmer for some time before we speak them, if we ever speak them at all. By the time we do express them, they've already made a home in our heart. We've grown accustomed to their presence. Jesus says, "You are the ones who justify yourselves in the eyes of men, but God knows your hearts" (Luke 16:15). He really does know our hearts.

OUR JUDGMENT OF OTHERS

WHEN I SPEAK ABOUT the sin of judgment, I am referring to what Jesus commands us not to do. I don't mean we cannot judge right or wrong actions or give correction. Paul says, "You are competent to judge cases and disputes" (1 Cor. 6:2). And Jesus says, "If your brother sins, rebuke him" (Luke 17:3).

Within the early Christian community, the believers recognized their responsibility to correct one another for wrongdoing, to call sin sin. We can indeed make judgments about another's actions. "Brothers, if someone is caught in a sin, you who are spiritual should restore him gently. But watch yourself, or you also may be tempted" (Gal. 6:1). If someone is being dishonest, unfaithful, or acting immorally, we should speak up, out of love and concern for them. But we need to be careful. The temptation is to take pride in ourselves, by making comparisons to the one who has fallen. In so doing, we deceive ourselves into thinking we are superior to others. And that's why Paul says that those who are spiritual should be the ones who seek out the other person.

In Romans 14, Paul asks, "You, then, why do you judge your brothers? Or why do you look down on your brothers?" (v. 10). He was pleading for the brethren to accept one another; he exhorted them to stop passing judgments on "disputable matters." Some were keeping the Jewish dietary laws and laws about the Sabbath and other special days. Paul's message was that if one person eats meat he does it for the Lord, if one abstains he also does it for the Lord.

In disputable matters we should always presume that what our brother or sister is doing, they are doing out of love for God. We cannot judge because only God knows a person's heart and "each of us will give an account of himself to God" (Rom. 14:12).

Being irritated, angry, or troubled by Stan's tardiness was not the problem. Irresponsible behavior we can judge as wrong. An emotional response is normal. The problem comes when our anger does not lead us to resolve the issue in love but rather leads us to separate from relationship by taking a superior position, to look down at, to label, to withdraw, to reject, or to condemn. The real lesson of our experience was that had Janet taken up a position of judgment toward Stan, she never would have received the grace God had for her. When we judge others, we separate ourselves from the grace which God wants to bring to us through that relationship.

The Greek word **krima** is translated in the New Testament as either judgment or condemnation, depending on the text. Understanding the connection between the two brought me to a new level of insight about what it means when Scripture says, "Do not judge." It means, "Don't reject someone else. Don't declare that person guilty. Don't give a verdict about someone and condemn him or her."

It is more than simply what we think about a person; it has to do with our relationship. We are commanded not to judge because apart from the grace of God our judgment leads to condemnation, not mercy.

We can be deceived into constantly looking at what's wrong in others or in the church, thinking it's "discernment" that we're receiving. We may think God has given us a particular insight so we can see how much someone needs Jesus. But it isn't really difficult to see how much others or the church needs more conversion, more of Jesus.

If God is truly giving us discernment, it is for a reason. The reason is not to take security in our superior knowledge, or to look down upon others, or to categorize them so we don't have to deal with them as real human beings. Our compassion for others should move us to repent of that very sin within us, as an expression of solidarity with others. We can take the opportunity to personally gain victory as well as pray for the mercy of God to be revealed to others as it has been to us.

JESUS AS JUDGE

J OHN 5:27 RECORDS Jesus' declaration about his authority
to judge. "And he has given him authority to judge because
he is the Son of Man." Later in that passage Jesus says, "I
judge only as I hear" (5:30).

Jesus was pointing out that his judgment is only in union
with the Father. He emphasized this for our sake, that we
would know that only God can judge. Only God is all merciful. When God judges me or you or his church, his judgment
is a demonstration of his mercy.

Sometimes we think these two words, **judgment** and
mercy, are contradictory. For us they might be; but for God
they're not. His judgments are merciful. Our judgments, apart
from grace, are not merciful; they're condemning.

In the eighth chapter of John, we read about a time when
Jesus was asked to judge someone:

> *The teachers of the law and the Pharisees brought in*
> *a woman caught in adultery. They made her stand*
> *before the group and said to Jesus, "Teacher, this*
> *woman was caught in the act of adultery. In the Law*
> *Moses commanded us to stone such women. Now what*
> *do you say?" They were using this question as a trap,*
> *in order to have a basis for accusing him. But Jesus*
> *bent down and started to write on the ground with his*
> *finger. When they kept on questioning him, he*
> *straightened up and said to them, "If any one of you*
> *is without sin, let him be the first to throw a stone at*
> *her." Again he stooped down and wrote on the ground.*
> (John 8:3-8)

Many scholars believe that Jesus was drawing symbols or words on the ground identifying their sins, which he well knew. Yet apparently they didn't catch on right away; they kept on questioning him. So he finally gave them a clue: "If any one of you is without sin, let him throw the first stone." Then he stooped down and wrote some more. (I don't know how long the list would have to get before *you* would turn and walk away, but if my sins were being written out, I think I would have walked away pretty soon!)

The passage continues: "At this, those who heard began to go away one at a time, the older ones first *[they were the wiser]*, until only Jesus was left, with the woman still standing there. Jesus straightened up and asked her, 'Woman, where are they? Has no one condemned you?'" (John 8:9-10). They weren't asking Jesus to judge the woman with mercy; they were looking for Jesus to condemn the woman. They wanted Jesus to judge her by human standards. Later, Jesus said, "You judge by human standards. I pass judgment on no one" (v. 15). They were asking Jesus to judge on one standard; according to the Law, she was guilty, condemned. (Based on these standards we are also condemned.) Jesus pointed out to them that they were all guilty, that they were all in their sin, and that they were all under condemnation. Consequently, what right did they have to cast a stone, to judge someone else with condemnation?

The story of the woman caught in adultery ends with this: "Jesus straightened up and asked her, 'Woman, where are they? Has no one condemned you?' 'No one, sir,' she said. 'Then neither do I condemn you,' Jesus declared. 'Go now and leave your life of sin'" (John 8:10-11). We have no idea whether or not the woman was repentant and ready to leave her life of sin. All we know is that Jesus was offering her mercy. His actions and his words were to save her, not to condemn her.

God doesn't condemn or reject us; our sins do. Jesus didn't need to condemn the woman. If she continued in her sins, her sins would do that. Romans 1:18-19 says, "The wrath of God is being revealed from heaven against all the godlessness and wickedness of men ... since what may be known about God is plain to them ... " As you read on in Romans 1, Paul speaks of how God acts in his wrath, which is to give the godless over to the sinful desires of their hearts. That is God's judgment—to give them over to their sins, the sins to which they choose to cling instead of God.

Paul described how the godless exchanged truth for a lie and worshiped created things instead of the Creator; everything became a perversion and their rebellion led to lives filled with wickedness, evil, greed and depravity (Rom. 1:29). As the Book of Proverbs says, "Adversity pursues a sinner, but the righteous will be rewarded by prosperity" (13:21). Problems will follow us in our judgments and our sins.

God's judgment is in the nature of our sin. He hands us over to our sins. Why? Because he loves us. Because when we discover what a mess we are, we're going to repent. He's calling us back.

The Scripture speaks about sowing and reaping. What you sow, you reap; that's a law. It's a spiritual principle. God's design is that when we do enter into sin, we reap back what we've sown, as a judgment, so that we might be called to repentance.

Ultimately, God's full wrath against our sin was poured out on the spotless Lamb for us. "For God did not appoint us to suffer wrath but to receive salvation through our Lord Jesus Christ. He died for us so that . . . we may live together with him" (1 Th. 5:9-10).

CHRIST'S MERCY COMPARED TO OUR JUDGMENTS

I SAIAH TELLS US that the Messiah will not judge by what he sees with his eyes or decide by what he hears with his ears, but by righteousness and justice (Is. 11:3). Our judgments are sometimes like those of the Pharisees who wished to stone the woman; they're based on deception and self-justification.

We attempt to justify ourselves by comparing ourselves to others. I've been doing that all my life. When I was about five years old, I was in the bathroom, thinking about heaven and hell. I was wondering if I was going to make it to heaven, because I was a little worried about hell. I said to myself, *I'm not that good, but I know I'm better than Louie, next door.* That gave me great comfort, because if *I* wasn't going to make it, I knew Louie wasn't going to make it either. At least I'd have somebody I knew there!

We do that all the time; we try to feel better about ourselves and our failings by comparing: "Oh, I'm terrible—but not as bad as so-and-so." We don't even look at ourselves to acknowledge what really is terrible. We are merely anxious to feel self-justified, which then gives us permission to go around condemning others. "Oh, look at that. Look at what they did. Did you hear what they said?" We want everyone to be in the mud with (or except) us.

Look again at the older brother in Luke's parable. He's obviously comparing his own righteousness to his brother's careless, overtly sinful lifestyle. He's making judgments based on comparisons. But, in reality, isn't he harboring the same sins in his heart: leaving, withholding his presence from the father, breaking the father's heart, being selfish, immature, rebellious, self-seeking?

When we judge one another, we are deceiving ourselves; we don't understand the true condition of our hearts. If we truly understood the condition of our hearts apart from Christ and his mercy, we would never judge (i.e., condemn) anyone.

Our judgments also tell us that we don't understand God's mercy toward us. When we judge, we're confirming that we haven't received his mercy.

A further Scripture brings this out, demonstrating that when we judge others we actually condemn ourselves.

You, therefore, have no excuse, you who pass judgment on someone else. For on whatever point you judge the other you are condemning yourself, because you who pass judgment do the same things. Now we know that God's judgment against those who do such things is based on truth, so when you, a mere man, pass judgment on them and yet do the same things, do you think you will escape God's judgment? (Rom. 2:1-3)

When we judge someone else we condemn ourselves, because the same sin is in us.

In her job as a nurse, my wife often comes home with horrifying stories of the effects of child abuse. My heart naturally wells up in judgment, hatred, and anger toward someone who would perpetrate such deeds. Hatred is in my heart. But 1 John 3:15 says that hatred is the same thing as murder. Can I judge the grace of God at work in the child abuser compared to the grace of God at work in me? Is that person's sin greater than mine? Objectively, yes. Subjectively... only God knows. Who am I to judge? Only God knows the heart.

Suppose somebody commits adultery and I say, "I've never committed adultery. How could somebody do something like that?" But have I ever lusted in my heart? Who am I to judge? Who am I to condemn and reject? Only God knows the heart. If I judge, I condemn myself. I'm demonstrating that I'm still in my sins, still under condemnation. If that sin is no longer in my heart, it is because of the mercy of God, because his love has covered that sin. He has cleansed it with his blood and set me free. If I am truly free of it, mercy is going to flow out of my heart, not judgment, because mercy has been shown to me. But when I judge, I declare before others and to myself that I'm not free of my sins, that I'm still walking in them.

I believe that our judgments are rooted in the fact that we walk under condemnation and not mercy; we still haven't accepted God's mercy for our lives. When we're walking under condemnation we have a choice about how to get out of it. We can turn to God and cry out for mercy, and trust in him, or we can turn to self-justification.

The apostle Paul says, "For there is therefore now no condemnation for those who are in Christ Jesus" (Rom. 8:1). If we're predestined to be formed into the likeness of the Son, if he would be the first of many brethren, how can we walk under condemnation? Let's not look at ourselves as our sins demand. Let's not look at others as their sins demand. Let's look at what God created. Let's look at our destiny, our call, our potential in Christ. Let us realize that Christ himself has given us his very own life; in him, we have been justified. We don't have to walk under condemnation. And since we're not under condemnation, we no longer have to judge others. Since mercy has been shown us, we too can show mercy. We will grasp God's heart for others if we will first allow God to deal with us and release his mercy into that area in which we are judging others.

God's View

GOD WANTS to take pleasure in you for all eternity. He wants you to see him. We can't see him through the lens of condemnation. We can't see others through the lens of condemnation.

I must confess that I've been judging people all my life. It has been pretty standard for me. Yet God has given me glimpses of freedom from judgment. When I was baptized in the Spirit in 1970, I remember walking down the college campus looking around at people passing by. They all looked different. Everything looked different. I felt free. I felt accepting. I wasn't comparing. I knew God loved me, and I freely loved everybody from my heart. It was just flowing. There wasn't any judgment or condemnation there. I experienced a glimpse of purity of heart, something that God has been working into me ever since.

I was once at an airport, and happened to be meditating on the Scriptures about passing judgment. I looked around and saw a very heavyset man enjoying a large ice cream cone. Usually in areas where we are weak, we tend to judge others more harshly, and I often have a problem with my eating habits. All of a sudden, I realized that I was looking at him without judgment. I was looking at him and thinking, *Wow, isn't it great to be free and simply enjoying life, rather than always being down on yourself about your problems?* I was looking around and seeing all the good in people. I thought, *Boy, that's not how I usually live. That's not how I usually look at people.*

Ask the Lord and he will give you a glimpse of what it's like to have a pure heart. If our hearts are pure, we can see the good, we can have mercy on people, and mercy will triumph over judgment. A pure heart is his promise to you—and you will see God.

Try this today: look at those around you without focusing on their faults. Notice the joy, freedom, and goodness in people, appreciating God's goodness in them. It's wonderful to see the mercy of God at work in others.

6

Uprooting
Deep-Seated Judgments

I'D LIKE TO EXAMINE a few ways in which the consequences of our judgments are measured back to us, and what we can do about it.

Jesus says, "Do not judge or you, too, will be judged; for in the same way you judge others, you will be judged. And with the measure you use it will be measured back to you" (Matt. 7:1-2). Often people experience repeating patterns of hurt, rejection, failure, and broken relationships. Why? Sometimes it's because there is a root of judgment in their lives. An old bitterness is getting measured back to them.

JUDGMENTS: OBVIOUS AND SUBTLE

SOME JUDGMENTS AND RESENTMENTS are obvious; you can pinpoint a crisis or a day that "set you off." You may have been unjustly fired from a job because somebody lied about you. Perhaps you were brought to court by a friend and felt betrayed. You may have been ripped off in an inheritance. Or maybe your teenage son robbed you to get drugs. Your judgment of these people may have an obviously condemning quality to it.

But some resentments—judgments or condemnations—are a little more subtle. They are not related to specific one-time events; they flow from deep, maybe even subconscious, roots. We may be convinced that these judgments are based on facts. Sometimes they are, but not always. You may say something like:

"When I was growing up, my dad never had time for me."

"My mom was always sick."

"My brothers and sisters got all the breaks."

"My boss hates me."

Are these statements really true—or are they actually old judgments that need to be broken?

A woman once told me about her father, a man who was rarely home when Sarah was growing up. He seemed to be always working.

Sarah remembered a specific conversation with him when she asked, "Daddy, would you stay home on Saturday, some Saturday—even one Saturday? Daddy, please. We need you." (Sarah was the overly responsible one in the family.)

His answer? "You need shoes."

When she asked him again, he said, "You need a coat."

As a child, Sarah couldn't verbalize what she thought in her heart. But a judgment was made: "My daddy doesn't love me, and he doesn't care for me. I'm not good enough. He doesn't want to be with me."

As time passed, Sarah grew unable to trust. She made a subconscious decision: "I can't expect care from people." Remembering this painful episode enabled her to understand and deal with her deeper emotional response. The judgment that she made of her father did not happen in that one conversation; it was a result of the relationship. Just like the parable/story genre, this one incident revealed a central truth about the relationship. The internal response Sarah had made to her father carried over into every relationship she ever had until she could see it and repent. Judgments hold us bound and keep coming back to us, causing problems.

How does it happen? I'll give you a somewhat simplistic way of understanding how it works. First, we don't receive love and acceptance. We feel hurt, and we respond as the sinful, "natural man"—not with the heart and mercy of God but with judgment. When somebody sins against us, we use it as an excuse not to love him or her. "I don't have to love her anymore; see what a terrible person she is?" We reject them, and our hearts become hardened.

Another response may be a bit different, with the same results. "This confirms that they don't love me. I'll try harder—and earn their love and acceptance." Instead of withdrawing from the relationship, we press in with expectations and demands for acceptance from others, setting ourselves up for further rejection.

Hardness of heart keeps us from receiving grace and mercy. We reject people and events and circumstances that God has brought into our lives ultimately for our benefit. For example, if we have consciously or subconsciously judged that our parents didn't love us, how can we believe that anybody can love us? After all, if you can't count on supposedly reliable parents, who's left to count on? We may not directly say this, but it's how we relate in life. Our hard-hearted judgment against our parents makes us reject what love they did have to offer us. As a result, we don't receive the love we need; and if we don't receive love, we don't have love to give. We're "stuck."

Hardness of heart also creates negative expectations that also make us stuck. People who judge expect to be judged—or they expect to fail, expect to be rejected or lonely or ignored. We often create our own world by how we look at things. If a child makes the judgment, "I've been rejected," the pattern continues; at every level, that person expects to be judged. He or she must constantly fight being rejected.

I've seen this pattern over and over again. One woman I know judged her parents at a young age, concluding that they didn't have any time for her. Because of that judgment, she resolved, "I'll take care of myself." And she did well. She was very successful in school, a leader of all kinds of clubs, mature in many ways. But into every relationship she carried the conviction that her needs would not be met. So she continually felt the need to be strong and take care of other people.

Some people who have experienced the pain of rejection and have responded with judgment are always challenging—even daring—others to accept them. And, of course, the others don't. This is the child in school who's always acting up, demanding attention. The attention he gets is salted with anger and frustration; it's far from the acceptance he seeks. But any attention can seem better than no attention.

Others try to earn acceptance, seeking to prove themselves, identifying themselves with what they do, becoming performance-oriented. Throughout the years, I have met many people who have sought to find acceptance in our community, or with me, by trying very hard to be the "perfect" community member. They've tried to do everything right—only to find out that there is no perfect community member, and our love and acceptance is not borne out of performance.

Others hold back in fear, not giving themselves freely to others, making acceptance and love difficult to receive. This was true of me. I have an older sister, Rita, whom I saw as very demanding. Two memories capture my response to her.

The first one happened when I was about five years old, when Rita was swinging a belt over my head. In response to my protest, she said, "Trust me, I won't hit you." For some reason she wanted to see how close she could get without hitting me; and, sure enough, I got it right in the face. My inner resolve: "I will never trust you again."

When I was six, I remember going to my room after getting the worst of another fight with Rita. In frustration and anger I determined that from that point on I would make a list of every incident so that I could get back at her when I was older.

Bitterness is unfulfilled revenge. I had allowed bitterness to take root in my heart. As we grew, our relationship bore the consequence of my sin. We were not very close. I would relate to her selfishly, wanting the relationship only on my own terms, protecting and isolating myself from her. Even in my late twenties when I was fervently seeking to live for God, I remember conversations in which I felt Rita was aggressively seeking more from our relationship. That put my insides into turmoil. I really wanted to respond to her warmly; I wanted things to be better, but my response was cold and distant. I dreaded being in a situation that was out of my control—vulnerable to the internal responses that our relationship provoked.

I could see what I was doing, and I didn't like it, but I didn't know what to do about it. For a while I rationalized, excusing my behavior based on our personality differences, based on "the way she was," or the way she didn't understand me. I even convinced myself that she wasn't aware of my lack of love toward her.

I couldn't articulate the problem, but I knew it was hard for me to give and receive love, not only in this relationship but with others. I expressed love by doing, by serving, by using my gifts to help, but I found it hard to share myself warmly and personally. Show me what to do, and I would do it; give me more to do, and I would feel better; but ask me to simply be me, and I didn't know how. This is the classic older brother, doing all that he was told, but having a heart of resentment toward his brother and an empty relationship with his father.

GOD'S LESSON THROUGH MY "OLDER" SON

THIRTEEN YEARS AGO, my mother came through Pennsylvania on her way to a pilgrimage to Rome and Israel. The night she stopped, she came down with spinal meningitis. She went into a coma for five weeks and was in the hospital for a year and a half. During this time, my stepfather was living with us, my aunt died, and our fourth child was born. To put it mildly, these were difficult days.

But if outward appearances were any indication, I thought we were doing all right under the circumstances. That is, until my five-year-old son started having problems, withdrawing and looking depressed. He was always out of sorts with his brothers, and nothing we did seemed to make things turn around for him.

For five years, we prayed, agonized, and sought the Lord. (Some of you may be praying and agonizing over situations right now that don't seem like they're ever going to end. They do.) In God's timing, in his mercy, he had a lesson for me about judgments and about matters of the heart.

Here's what happened. In God's perfect timing, my son, now a ten-year-old, was given psychological tests at school. He had to write out answers to certain questions. One of his answers referred to a little boy and a baby being born.

Considering the context of the question, it became clear to us that his problems were rooted back to that time in our family's life when his younger brother was born. In another of the answers, he wrote about a little boy who ran away. I thought and prayed about that; and, through a book[‡] I was then reading, the Lord gave me conviction and understanding that although my son had never actually run away physically, he had run away in his heart.

"Lord," I said, "we've been praying for five years. I don't know how to minister to kids. I don't know how to bring them to healing. Help us."

[‡] John and Paula Sandford, *The Transformation of the Inner Man* (So. Plainfield, NJ: Bridge Publishing, Inc., 1982), esp. pp. 237-266. I am very grateful to the Sandfords for their insights on judgments, which have greatly enhanced my observations in this chapter.

Two mornings later, my ten-year-old son was involved in a conflict with one of his brothers right before family prayer—the same insolvable, unworkable, unreasonable problems. What seemed plain to most family members was perceived very differently by him. He was looking at issues from a different perspective, interpreting right and wrong according to what he felt being right and wrong meant. *Am I loved or not?* Correcting a situation often ended in hurt, or a stubborn refusal to admit any wrongdoing. This morning was typical. It ended with hurt.

But this time I had a new perspective, and I fully expected God to work in the situation. I said, "Son, what's the matter? What's really bothering you?"

He said, "Dad, you just don't have any time for me."

Over the last several years, I had heard him say that six or seven times. And every time I responded by saying, "I have more time for you than I have for the other children; I'm always spending time with you." But now I understood something. I understood that it was a judgment that he had made five years before: "My daddy doesn't have any time for me." And, back then, I truly hadn't given him the time he deserved. But ever since then, he was relating to me out of that hurt and judgment. No matter how much time I gave him, it was never enough.

Instead of trying to explain and reason with him about how much time we actually spent with him, this time I knew I was speaking to the five-year-old. I simply said, "Son, would you forgive me for not having enough time with you, for not taking the time with you that you need? I really want to spend time with you."

I asked him to forgive me, and he did.

Then I said, "Son, did you ever feel like running away?"

"No, Dad."

"Did you ever run away in your heart?"

"No."

But then a light bulb went on. "Yes," he said, "I did."

"Son, would you come back home, now?"

And he did.

I was overwhelmed with the same joy that the prodigal son's father must have experienced. And, in a way, I was really welcoming home the older brother. My son had been with me in person; but I hadn't realized how far away he'd gone. In his heart, he had left, and he had been suffering because of it. We hugged, and I realized that my son had been gone for a long time. When I held him, I held that little boy again, the boy I'd had so much fun with, playing and holding.

A time of grace like that doesn't solve everything, but it sure did break a logjam and help move our family in the right direction.

That's the pattern of judgments. When we pull back from those whom God has provided in our life, we reject them, we judge them, and we hold ourselves bound. We're the ones who suffer until we get free. Our judgments can hold us bound not only emotionally but physically and spiritually as well.

Open to God's Healing

Shortly after I encountered the Lord Jesus in my den in 1970, I began to notice that many people focused on God the Father in prayer. Since I had not yet experienced

God as my Father, I somehow felt that praying to the Father was second best. After all, I thought, Jesus is Lord, and we have received the Spirit of Jesus.

Gradually the truth dawned on me. Something was missing. As I began to seek to know God as my Father, I had to face the truth that something was missing in my relationship with my father. This was difficult because I did not have painful memories.

The problem was not what had happened but what had *not* happened—what was missing. I had not experienced the personal, intimate, emotional aspects of our relationship.

As my seeking grew intense, God provided someone who prayed for me, asking God the Father to come and be my father, filling the void that was in me. That was a life-changing moment. A part of me that had long been dead came to life. A new level of freedom entered my life. Having been very quiet most of my life, I found myself talking more freely than ever before.

Following this experience of God's healing power, I began to seek healing for many of the things that caused me pain, and many of the fears and insecurities that would rise up in my life. Much of this type of prayer focuses on the love that we have not received in life. But it wasn't until I shifted my focus that I experienced a far more profound freedom and a greater maturity. The shift involved taking responsibility and repenting for my sinful responses to these hurtful experiences.

We all must come to grips with the fact that we are responsible for how we've responded to the circumstances of our lives. Yes, it is good to be healed of life's hurts, to receive

God's love into ever new areas of our life, but real freedom often comes only through forgiveness and repentance.

Some time ago, while receiving prayer for healing, I had a picture, a sense, about the womb. I casually told the person praying with me, "I just had this sense about the womb." He put his hand on my chest and commanded my spirit to be healed. Immediately, I dropped to the floor in a fetal position. I remember thinking, *Uh oh, what's happening here?* My hands came up to my mouth, and an incredible pain and wailing came out of me.

A part of me was observing and thinking, *Is this really happening?* God was releasing something in me that had been with me all my life, something that had happened to me when I was in the womb. As the wailing stopped, I began saying over and over again, "I love you, Mommy. I love you, Daddy."

I suddenly realized that for all these years I had been praying about the love I didn't receive. But this experience showed me that from the very moment of my birth I wasn't trusting in the love my parents had for me. I was withholding my love from them—holding back—because of hurt.

Of course, none of us has fully received from our parents as much love as we've needed. But now I saw that my parents had given me a lot of love, yet I couldn't receive it, because I was trying to protect myself. Truly, we are formed in our mother's womb!

The pattern of my sinful response to life's situations (e.g., my sister) had already begun in the womb. Yes, I needed to be released from the pain, but the greater damage came from my *response* to it. I needed to take full responsibility, repent, and decide to love, starting with my parents. This experience led me to a greater freedom. I chose my parents as the perfect parents for me.

Allow me to explain.

God had chosen my parents. He knew what he was doing. He knew their weaknesses and sins. He also knew my personality and the plan he would have for my life. If we are filled with bitter judgment and regret, we have not yet come through to the point of seeing how the hand of God can take the most negative experiences and make them useful for his kingdom—and a blessing for us. Most children find themselves during adolescence going through some level of rejection of their parents. Maturity comes as we grow past our hurt and loss and begin to be grateful for the parents we have been given. To embrace them for who they are is to come to a deeper place of self-acceptance, to choose what God has chosen. This principle is true for every difficult relationship or situation that God has allowed to enter our lives. To judge another is to reject what God has chosen.

WHERE ARE YOU?

O UR JUDGMENTS produce judgments, the same measure, measured back to us. We experience the consequence of our judgments coming back to us—which is actually God's mercy for us, because these very recurring, painful patterns propel us on in Christ. When our sins come back to us, they move us further in seeking more and wanting more of Christ's redemption and grace.

At some point, the pain you feel may be so intense that you might vow never to let yourself be hurt again. Yet the

Lord wants you to give him permission to bring up a painful scenario. You see, as we turn to God and humbly ask "Why?", that's when we should remember that his judgment reveals his mercy. How? When we sin, God's heart breaks for us. We're going to be coming under his judgment of our sin, and he's reaching out to save us.

A scenario might well be repeating itself in your life so that you can have an opportunity to respond out of God's grace—to repent from the patterned response within and choose to love. Here is an opportunity to realize that you are new in Christ; you've been covered by his blood. His life is in you, wanting to be released more fully in you and through you. Because of him, you no longer need to control everything, you can trust him who holds all things in his hands. You don't have to relate to people the way you want them to be or need them to be. You can relate to people for who they are.

Remember, we're inclined to see others according to the attitudes and expectations of our own hearts. We can't see God if we don't have a pure heart. We can't see others for who they are if we don't have a pure heart.

If you identify in some way with some of these words about deep-seated judgment, the first thing you need to do is to recognize that you are responsible for the sinful response to difficult situations that has caused a hardening of your heart.

The second thing you need to do is to repent of the judgments in your heart and ask the Lord to break the patterns and structures that have been built up in your mind—the patterns that expect judgment and hurt. "Do not conform any longer to the pattern of this world, but be transformed by the renewing of your mind" (Rom. 12:12). Repent for making a home for bitterness and resentment. Repent for walking in unforgiveness, justifying your position by the judgments you have made. Repent for your hidden judgments of God, the ways you have failed to believe in his love for you in difficult times. When we reject God's provision for us, we reject God.

Finally, I ask you to agree with God. Agree to accept his provision. Receive his grace through the people whom God has chosen to grace you. Pursue the Lord relentlessly until you are walking in forgiveness and able to accept and love your parents, that brother or sister, pastor, prayer group leader, or friend.

Often it is the very person we blame for messing up our lives that God is using as an instrument to reveal our impure hearts and break our pride. The older brother saw his younger brother as the enemy, when really the enemy was within his own heart. Those who oppose us are often servants of God raised up to humble us. You can see this throughout the Old Testament, as Israel's "enemies" opposed them to turn them back to the Lord.

Jesus tells us to love our enemies and pray for those who persecute us. We know that forgiveness is complete and bitterness is gone when we can pray a sincere blessing on a "thorny" person or group without demanding some sort of prerequisite for the blessing. We know that forgiveness is complete when we not only stop wishing them harm but also pray that God will bless and prosper them and use them in a greater way than ourselves. We know that we have repented when we begin to be grateful for the revelation that the plank is in our own eyes, and that we are seeing a speck of dust in our brother's.

WHEN YOU CAN'T LET GO

M AYBE YOU HAVE YOUR DOUBTS about whether you'll be led to freedom from your long-term resentment or bitterness toward your "younger brother"—perhaps one who has not returned home with a contrite heart but who remains bitter and wanton and wounded, a thorn in your flesh.

Maybe it's that betrayal by someone you trusted that has crippled you. We know that in wartime one of the most difficult things for a family is to hear that their soldier has been killed by "friendly fire."

We can talk about the love of God. We can believe it and even feel it. But the love of God does not truly advance until it meets the sin and evil in our hearts and in the world around us. Until there is an encounter, victory has not come.

I think of the apostle Thomas as he's described after Jesus' resurrection. Thomas had been wounded and disillusioned. He might have felt abandoned and disappointed. He lacked trust in his Lord and probably wondered whether the good plans he had for the future were over. *This is not the way it's supposed to be,* may have been his cry, even as the rest of his community was rejoicing in victory, saying, "We have seen the Lord."

Thomas's response speaks to me not only of unbelief but of deep anger and challenge: "Unless I see the nail marks in his hands and put my finger where the nails were, and put my hand into his side, I will not believe it" (John 20:25).

Perhaps you can imagine how Thomas felt. Have you ever felt so much pain that you resented somebody sharing the truth with you? What you really wanted to say is, "You don't understand how much it hurts." Thomas was saying, "Your witness is not good enough. I can't let go of this pain just because you say you've seen the Lord. I need more than that. I won't believe until . . ."

I'm not sure that Thomas really understood what he was asking for. Many of us might have asked for Jesus to come and hold us, or to give us a word to stand on, or to comfort us, or take away the pain. Thomas asked to touch the wounds, the wounds that speak of Jesus' love and mercy. Through these very wounds, the Lamb's blood flowed to save and set us free.

Yes, we want to be like Jesus, but do we want to embrace the wounds of love?

A week later Jesus stood among his disciples and said:

"Peace be with you!" Then he said to Thomas, "Put your finger here; see my hands. Reach out your hand and put it into my side. Stop doubting and believe." (John 20:26-27)

It took a week, but the Lord came to Thomas and through his falling, his humbling, Thomas was brought to a powerful rising. Can you imagine what it would be like to take your finger and put it into Jesus' wounded hands and place your hand into his side? To touch the very wounds that saved you? To come that close to him in his suffering and redemption, simply because you asked to be there? Thomas was given the opportunity to touch Jesus intimately, where

Jesus was pierced for Thomas's transgressions (Is. 53:5). And Thomas then responded, "My Lord and my God!" (John 20:28).

As we struggle to forgive and to love, we have the opportunity to join with the Savior in his suffering and to share with him in his glory. As we "fall" and give ourselves over to love those who have acted as our enemies—even if it is simply through prayer on their behalf—the redemption of Christ is manifest through us. The kingdom of God advances.

I believe that if you truly ask to see the wounds of Jesus, the suffering of Christ on your behalf, you will see him. Thomas's story holds out for us a promise of victory. As we seek the Lord, as the merciful suffering of Christ overflows in our lives, the Lamb that was slain for our sins is revealed. And in that revelation comes his peace and our declaration, "My Lord and my God!"

Years after my sister and I had both come into a personal relationship with the Lord Jesus, we were at a family dinner together. She asked those of us gathered to forgive her for all the things she had done to hurt or harm us, intentionally or unintentionally, as she was growing up. We all forgave her. Her request prompted others at the table to follow suit and ask Rita for forgiveness.

But suddenly I was stuck. I had been believing a lie and now it was exposed. I did not have it within me to ask for forgiveness—because I had focused on the wrong that had been done to me (considering as insignificant the wrong I had done to her).

I could hide no longer. The problem that we were having wasn't so much *our* problem but *my* problem. This was my moment of humbling that led me to a powerful rising.

The day eventually came when I was fully able to take responsibility for the way I had acted and felt toward Rita. Without excuse, I confessed my sin, and, from a place of helplessness, I asked God to forgive me and deliver me. Just as Jesus came to Thomas behind locked doors, I experienced Jesus come into an area of my life long locked up. And he set me free from bitterness.

We, like Thomas, are invited to touch the power of the Servant's wounds, his suffering and death, and find our freedom in the risen Lord.

Recently Rita and I worked together on a weekend conference in which we gave testimony together to the power of God's love in our relationship. As the weekend progressed, I couldn't help but chuckle as I was attracted to, and admired, qualities in Rita that used to repel me. At one time I dreaded her visits. Now I hoped to have someone just like her to work with in our community!

Although Rita told me that she had always experienced my support through the years, the Lord had now melted my heart of ice and given us a new relationship. We are now sister and brother in Christ, by choice. Love that has persevered through the testing is something that is very precious indeed.

7

Worthy or Unworthy?

I AM NO LONGER WORTHY TO BE CALLED YOUR
SON; MAKE ME LIKE ONE OF YOUR HIRED SERVANTS.

— The younger brother

CHRISTIANS OFTEN STRUGGLE with big "Who am I?" questions. Servant or son? Worthy or unworthy?

The "Who am I?" questions were probably not on the mind of the older brother, who was quite sure he had the answers. *I'm the older, faithful son, thank you.* But I'd like us to imagine his story beyond what's told in the Scriptures, envisioning a time when he came to his senses and ultimately realized he didn't have answers.

When he asked the questions, what answers would he have found? Was he worthy of the father's love? How did he see himself? On what was he to base his identity?

In Luke's Gospel, Jesus tells the basic story of the two brothers all over again, in a different context.

Two men went up to the temple to pray, one a Pharisee and the other a tax collector. The Pharisee stood up and prayed about himself: "God, I thank you that I am not like other men—robbers, evildoers, adulterers— or even like this tax collector. I fast twice a week and give a tenth of all I get." But the tax collector stood at a distance. He would not even look up to heaven, but beat his breast and said, "God, have mercy on me, a sinner." I tell you that this man, rather than the other, went home justified before God. For everyone who exalts himself will be humbled, and he who humbles himself will be exalted. (Luke 18:10-14)

Consider the two men Jesus is describing here.

One was blinded to the truth, justifying himself before God by looking upon himself, comparing himself to others, and boasting before God of his sacrificial lifestyle. He had not come to the temple to bow before the presence of God but to stand before others. He seemed more conscious of himself and the tax collector than the presence of God.

The other character, the tax collector, came before the Lord humbly recognizing his unworthiness yet focused on the God of mercy in whose presence he stood. He stood at a distance and did not even look up to heaven. Jesus commended this man, saying *he* was the one who went home justified. The man who came before God as unworthy went home worthy. He who humbled himself before God was the one whom God exalted.

Luke tells yet another story, an event in Jesus' life, in which the elders came to Jesus and pleaded with him to come and heal a centurion's servant. A centurion was a Roman soldier with some clout, an important man. The Jewish elders said to Jesus, "This man deserves to have you do this, because he loves our nation and has built our synagogue" (Luke 7:4-5). "So," Luke writes, "Jesus went with them."

He was not far from the house when the centurion sent friends to say to him: "Lord, don't trouble yourself, for I do not deserve to have you come under my roof. That is why I did not even consider myself worthy to come to you. But say the word, and my servant will be healed. . . ." When Jesus heard this, he was amazed at him, and turning to the crowd following him, he said, "I tell you, I have not found such great faith even in Israel." (Luke 7:6-7,9)

Worthy? Unworthy? Did this man have a bad self-image? An identity crisis?

The whole "Who am I?" issue is well illustrated by a recent experience I had at a church service.

We were singing one of my favorite hymns, "Amazing Grace." To my shock, they had changed the words: "Amazing grace, how sweet the sound that saved a *soul* like me"! What? John Newton had written of the amazing grace that had saved a *wretch* like him—a real younger, prodigal-son-type wretch, who had made his living trading and shipping slaves. But no, they had changed the words because it's not fashionable for people—Christians or non-Christians—to denigrate themselves and see themselves as wretched sinners.

Several times, as I've spoken on the topic of being unworthy of God's love, I've sensed a confusion and resistance on the faces before me. Many are not comfortable with the thought of being a "wretch, saved by grace." They've spent a lifetime working to bolster their sagging self-esteem; they don't need the church telling them they're unworthy of God's grace. Others are still-stuck older brothers, feeling secure in their own righteousness.

And that's only part of the story. Another segment of the Christian world is continually weeping and wailing, feeling condemnation that is not of God. They're always thoroughly convinced that they're wretches.

Let's try to sort out the truth from the lies and identify what our identity truly is in Christ.

UNWORTHY APART FROM CHRIST

A GOOD STARTING PLACE is the familiar, foundational scripture: "all have sinned and fall short of the glory of God" (Rom. 3:23). This is a powerful declaration of the truth of our situation. We will never grasp the significance of sin unless we realize the significance of falling short of the glory of God.

The glory of God includes his attributes and his power revealed through his creation and his mighty acts. In whatever God does, there is a manifestation of himself, his person, his character, his brightness and splendor. We were destined not only to see that glory, but also to share in it, to manifest it. We were created for his glory. We were created to enter into the eternal love of God.

Yet, because of sin, we have fallen short. One of the Greek words for sin used in the New Testament is **hamartia**. It literally means "to miss the mark." Knowing what we're aiming at, knowing what the target is, enables us to appreciate the significance and reality of sin. It is meaningless activity to take an arrow and shoot it randomly, without thought. (Dangerous, too!) Only by taking aim at something does a sense of purpose arise. Only then can we properly measure our development as a marksman.

To sin means that we have missed the mark with our lives. We were destined for the glory of God, and we have fallen short. We were destined to draw our own identity and purpose for existence from God's identity and purpose. We were destined to manifest him in our lives—his character, his power, and his Spirit. We were destined to know the Father through the Son. Sin reveals that man is searching for meaning and identity in activities, achievements, wealth, pleasure—things that may be good in and of themselves, gifts of our Father, but which were never meant to be a substitute for the glory of God.

Apart from faith in Christ, we find ourselves starved for acceptance and affirmation. Our human relationships, no matter how numerous and full, cannot meet our deepest needs. We are like paupers begging for crumbs, judging the value of our lives by how others respond to us.

We would be hopeless if not for Jesus, the only one who did not fall short of the glory of God. When Jesus was crucified, the curtain in the Jewish temple was torn, signifying that the wall separating us from the glory of God had been torn. Paul tells us that apart from Christ our minds are dull and our hearts are covered with a veil (2 Cor. 3:14). We cannot see clearly unless we turn to Christ, who reveals the glory of God. "The Son is the radiance of God's glory and the exact representation of his being, sustaining all things by his powerful word" (Heb. 1:3).

THE AUTHOR OF OUR FAITH KNEW HIS IDENTITY

THOUGH WE HAVE ALL missed the mark, falling short of our identity, Jesus hit the mark perfectly. Luke tells us about a very revealing moment in the life of Jesus as a twelve-year-old. The young boy asked his parents (who had been anxiously searching for him), "Why were you searching for me? Didn't you know I had to be in my Father's house?" (Luke 2:49). These first recorded words of Jesus reveal that he had set his sights on his Father and his Father's house. His last words on the cross were also directed to his Father: "Father, into your hands I commit my spirit," he called out with a loud voice (Luke 23:46). Jesus' aim was the same as it had been for all eternity: to love his Father and to glorify his name (John 12:28).

Jesus' total being, his very existence, was defined in relationship to his Father. The nature of this love was a self-giving, self-surrendering love. When Jesus died on the cross it wasn't something strange or abnormal to the character of God. It flowed from his very identity, his very nature. "Greater love has no one than this, that he lay down his life for his friends" (John 15:13).

The image we have of Jesus crucified is the clearest picture of the eternal, self-giving love of the Son, through whom we find our worthiness and our identity. We have been redeemed by his sacrificial death and glorious resurrection so that we can participate intimately in a love relationship, by the power of the Holy Spirit, as members of the very family of God.

Jesus never lost sight of the target. Hebrews 12:2 reminds us that Jesus endured the cross, scorning its shame, for the joy that was set before him. Jesus looked beyond the cross and its shame to the glory of sitting down at the right hand of the throne of God. In that same verse in Hebrews, we are called to fix our eyes on Jesus, the author and perfecter of our faith. We are called to take aim and make the person of Jesus our single target, that we might be joined with him in his abandonment before the Father.

WORTHY IN CHRIST

OUR GREAT VALUE—given to us in creation, distorted through sin—is ours again in its fullness through the redeeming work of Christ. On the cross, Christ dies for us, breaks the wall of separation, and reconciles us to God. Through faith and baptism, we join Christ in his death and pass with him through death into life in his resurrection.

Our great value, our worthiness, is a gift. It is not something we can earn. "While we were yet sinners, Christ died for us" (Rom. 5:8). Our good works, our long prayers, our years of service, can never earn us one drop of our Savior's blood. We will never deserve God's love; and yet, wretches that we are, he pours his love upon us as a gift. It is a gift we must choose to receive—with humility, reverence, and awe, always aware that we, though made worthy, are unworthy.

Separating Two Kinds of Unworthiness

I N THE GOSPEL STORIES at the beginning of this chapter—
the parable of the tax collector and the Pharisee, and the
healing of the centurion's servant—the unworthiness
esteemed by Jesus was clearly a heartfelt awe and reverence,
the "unworthiness" of mortal man approaching the glory of
God. He is not esteeming either man for chronically denigrat-
ing himself in the presence of other people.

There is no reason to believe that the centurion—a highly
respected, godly man in a position of military authority—had
a bad self-image. There is no reason to think that he felt
unworthy in the presence of others.

I've run into people who live day in and day out with
these thoughts: "I'm so insignificant; there is no purpose to
my life." "I'm no good." "I'm just a miserable sinner; there is
no hope for me."

This is not humility before the Lord but a spirit of
unworthiness that is a corruption of genuine humility. This
sense of worthlessness is an insult to God the Creator and to
Jesus, who found us valuable enough to give his life for us.

For these people, who struggle to see their own value,
their own mortality, I want to return to a few points I made
in Chapter 6, on uprooting deep-seated judgments. I spoke
of judgments we make of others—not seeing others as God
sees them—and of responding to circumstances and events
and personalities by being blind to the way God sees us.

One day my wife Janet and I were discussing a family
issue. At one point I began to react to her very defensively
and abruptly. As a result, the conversation deteriorated and

ended. Late that night, when I had a chance to be quiet before the Lord, I realized that what I was reacting to was not something Janet was saying but something I was hearing: "It's always your fault." It seemed as if I'd been hearing that all my life. Not recognizing what I was listening to, I tended to feel overly responsible and guilty when things didn't go well. (Reacting to this voice may well have contributed to my traveling the route of the older brother, trying to fix everything through my efforts and works.)

The voice I was listening to was not the voice of the loving Father, beckoning me into his arms. It was the "accuser of the brethren" (Rev. 12:10). From that deceiving pattern, the devil had a place from which to attack me.

It's as if the devil sees an area of darkness and says, "I'm going to use this against you, to bring you down. I'm going to accuse you until you are so preoccupied with yourself and so discouraged that you won't be able to go before the Lord in true worship."

Unless that area of my life is brought into the light of God's love, the devil has a right to accuse me. I can picture God telling the devil, "You have permission to use this against my son, until he comes to me with it. The pressure you put on him will enable him to see the lie and bring it to me. Through this, Jesus and the glory of his cross will be revealed, and you will know defeat because Neal belongs to me."

God can use such recurring thought patterns of unworthiness to show us who and where the enemy is. The enemy is not our parents or our second-grade school teacher or our spouse; the enemy works inside us, in our responses to others which God wants to bathe with grace and use for his glory.

Many deal with the spirit of unworthiness by seeking a bigger sense of "self." What they actually need is a bigger sense of God. As Jesus said, it is as we lose our life that we find it. It is not that we need greater self-confidence; we need to give ourselves over to confidence in God, the source of our true identity.

We don't need to overcome this sense of unworthiness as much as we need to admit it, believe that our Lord has overcome it, and live our lives standing not on the lie but on the truth of who Jesus is, the One who lives in us. We need to act on the truth, claim our relationship with him, and walk in obedience to God.

WORTHY OR UNWORTHY?

U PON MY RETURN from the 1985 Signs and Wonders conference in California, our community began to experience a powerful move of the Holy Spirit. Much of what I had experienced—deep repentance of sin, a return to my first love, renewed faith in the power of the Lord to heal and set the captives free—was being experienced by most of us.

With a desire to share my experience as fully as possible, we decided to gather together for a weekend to watch a series of videotapes from the conference. We invited everyone we knew to join us. To our surprise, several hundred people showed up, filling the room to capacity. Many came with deep needs—not simply seeking to learn, but hoping that God would do something in their lives. As the first video was coming to a close, and I was about to stand up and ask the Lord to come and work in our midst, I caught a glimpse of my true condition. *If God doesn't show up and manifest his*

Glory, I have nothing to give to these people. I don't even have anything to say. The words of Jesus were never so real to me: "Apart from me you can do nothing" (John 15:5).

The Lord did reveal his Glory to us. Many experienced the love of God leading them to repentance and an empowering by the Holy Spirit. Others had the opportunity to manifest the compassion of Jesus as they prayed for others through the laying on of hands. This compassion enabled many to bring into the light areas of pain that had long been buried. A number of people were healed physically. One woman was quite dramatically healed of a serious back problem, another stopped stuttering for the first time in over twenty years. The Lord had indeed come to us in very special ways, revealing his Glory.

For three days after the conference, I wept every time I thought about it. His love came so close that it hurt. It hurt because there was nothing in me that deserved his love and a lot that would disqualify me from it. It was a hurt that felt good, because it was both death to my life and life in him. It was both a deep sense of unworthiness and a revelation of how he has made me worthy.

So which is it? Are you worthy or are you unworthy? The answer is

YES!

8

The Father's Heart

MY SON, YOU ARE ALWAYS WITH ME, AND EVERY-
THING I HAVE IS YOURS.

— The father to the older brother

IN THE PARABLE ABOUT the two brothers, the one constant in the story is the father's love—for both children, the rigid and the raucous. The story of the older brother isn't complete without looking at the heart of the father, that is, our heavenly Father.

As we reflect and reveal the Father's love, what does it mean for us in our relationship with him? What does it mean for us in our relationships with one another?

The parable of the two brothers is about the family of God—God's generous self-giving love and his children's efforts to be in control. The parable is a contrast between the love of the father and the "love" of the sons—love that has been corrupted. The root of this corruption is not found in hate, which is the opposite of love, but in control, which disguises itself as love.

THE PHANTOM'S STORY

THE NIGHT BEFORE I BEGAN writing this chapter, I attended a musical production of *The Phantom of the Opera*. The story is about a man who, because of a gross physical deformity, has spent his life in isolation and hiding behind a mask, a symbol of his deception. Never having known love, he has none to give. Stealing away to an opera house, he presents himself to a young chorus girl, Christine, as an Angel of Music, sent to be her guardian and teacher.

By singing to her in her sleep, he enters her mind hypnotically, using his music to pull and control this young woman whom he thinks he loves. Another man, Raoul, also loves the young woman, who is vulnerable and mourning the loss of her father. And as she experiences Raoul's authentic love, she sees the corruption in the "Phantom's" soul. Realizing the danger she is in, she longs to be free of his influence and marry Raoul.

Once again she is captivated by the Phantom and taken to his hidden chamber. She has removed his mask and uncovered his hideous deformity, and now she will expose his soul.

Having captured Raoul, the Phantom demands that Christine choose to stay with him and save him from his solitude, or leave and watch him kill the one she loves. She chooses neither. Her choice is to call on God's help. She moves toward the Phantom and kisses him to let him know he is not alone. She expresses love and acceptance toward the horror of this soul. She offers him a type of salvation.

The story is a tragedy. He releases Raoul and sends Christine away with him, leaving several questions. Was it that her affection was too threatening, because he really did not seek love but control? Or was it that having been shown love for the first time, he then makes his first loving act in releasing her? In the end, he was left to die. Did he die in his own hell? Or did he die at peace having acted out of love for the first time?

For me, the most profound aspect of the play was the evil manifested in the Phantom's attempt to possess the young woman. Out of his own deep human need and Christine's obvious vulnerability (need), they are both opened to the deception of control. In this case the controlling enticement was beautiful music, corrupted for unhealthy purposes.

LUKE'S STORY

L ET'S RETURN to Luke's parable: "There was a man who had two sons. The younger one said to his father, 'Father, give me my share of the estate'" (Luke 15:11). What is the son doing? Making demands. Taking control—at any cost. He viewed his inheritance as his property. He took what he could get and left everything to do it his way.

The older brother worked to get, to possess, to control by manipulation. He was probably feeling pretty good after his younger brother left home. He didn't have to compete with his brother anymore. He probably had a greater measure of control. He knew his responsibilities and did them. Then one day his worst fears came true: the brother came home. He got the fatted calf. He got the party, the ring...for what? For ripping off his father? For irresponsibility? For a sin-filled lifestyle? For doing whatever he felt like doing? For doing all the things the older brother wanted to do but wouldn't dare?

I can almost hear his soul crying out, "After all my work, he won." His anger was now revealed. He refused to celebrate. He poured out his bitterness. His cover was blown. His motivations for being good were exposed, his secrets known. Though he seemed to have loved the father, had he really? Or was it love corrupted? Had he been trying to buy the father's love to fill his own need and insecurity?

CONTROL AND RELATIONSHIPS

THIS SPIRIT OF CONTROL—rampant still today—is rooted in fear and in need. Fear of rejection, of hurt, of facing one's humanity and lack of self-sufficiency. In our need, we distort true love.

Are our Christian leaders more concerned about bringing their brothers and sisters to maturity in Christ or about creating a climate that promotes dependency? When dependency becomes a relationship's security, the one with the upper hand says, "They can't hurt or reject me, because they need me." Parents do this with their children. Leaders do it with followers, especially in the church, as people often come to the church body at very needy points in their lives. A leader may not be aware of how much he likes to be needed, or how much she actually does to maintain the control and encourage the dependency.

These subtle manipulations are distortions of love, disrespectful of a person's individuality. Have you heard of a father pressuring a son to be the football player he always wanted to be, regardless of the child's desire? Or of a church that demands its pastor to be like some world-class preacher, when his gifts are more pastoral? Or of a leader who pressures the group to be like himself or like some other group, inconsistent with the group's nature?

We can manipulate through emotions, controlling children or adults by making them feel guilty. We can manipulate through prooftexting Scripture or claiming that we speak for God. Distorted love takes good things, as the Phantom took music, and corrupts them. The corrupted "instruments" may include emotions, logic, reason, sexual attraction, authority, religious experience, and desire.

The manipulation and pressure often work—at least for a while—because the need to control is often complemented by the need to please. But when we take it upon ourselves to meet our needs or the needs of others apart from the grace that comes through entrusting ourselves to God, we are living in deception.

At this point the apostle Paul might say, "Who will rescue me?" Only the love of the Father, revealed through the Son, can deliver us.

MY STORY

WHEN MY FIRST CHILD was born, a very wise woman told me that I was going to learn a great deal about the Father's love through being a parent. My oldest son is twenty-one now, and I can only say, "How right she was." Letting go is one of the marks of that amazing love. Our Father's love is so strikingly pure precisely because it isn't rooted in need; it is pure and unconditional and giving.

The last few years of my parenting have been marked by the struggle to let go of my sons, particularly the oldest, the first to cross the bar to manhood. Almost daily we struggled with the challenge of deciding how much responsibility and freedom he should be given. When he first went away to college, the geographical distance brought a certain sadness, but it marked the beginning of something full of great potential. His leaving home was the outward expression of the long, internal process of release. The time had come for him to experience the freedom for which we had been preparing him. Releasing the ones we love is one of the marks of the Father's love.

ADAM'S STORY

THE FATHER'S HEART is one that gives life, not one that takes it or forces it. The Father is one who invites— with utter respect for the individual. He bestows dignity and will not take it away.

We see the pattern in Genesis. God is revealed as Father to Adam. He provides Adam an inheritance and work to do, bestows authority on him, even "finds" him a wife. Together, Adam and Eve share equally in this sonship, which is the very relationship we have with the Father through the eternal Son, Jesus.

God did with Adam and Eve what a good Jewish father would do with his children. He instructed them in the way they should go, and then he let them experience freedom. But Adam and Eve had a "better" idea. They sought to take control, to withdraw from the intimate loving relationship they had with the One who really was in control.

Once his children made the wrong choice, God allowed them to see the full consequences of their actions, the awful prospect of living apart from him and his provision. He was not—and is not—a doting father, trying to overprotect his children, keeping them from the true freedom of maturity. He sees their dignity and wants them to come to maturity.

As we consider the parable of the prodigal, how did the father respond to the younger son's request (demand) to take his share of the estate? Luke says simply, "So [the father] divided his property between [the sons]" (Luke 15:12).

For a father to grant this request would have been shocking in Jesus' day. Yet the younger son, knowing something of his father's generosity, asked "for the moon" anyway. The father gave him a share in the property and with it the son received a new freedom to choose. The younger son had come of age. It was time for him to grow up.

JESUS' STORY

THOUGH HE GRANTS free will to his children, God our Father does not turn his back. In fact, "while we were yet sinners," he chose to make provision to give himself fully for our redemption, by giving his eternal Son. In Jesus, the Father ran to us while we were still a long way off, threw his arms around us, and kissed us.

The deeper meaning of this family parable is found in the life, death, and resurrection of the Son of God. The love of the Father is to give. He "so loved the world that he gave his one and only Son, that whoever believes in him shall not perish but have eternal life" (John 3:16). The desire of the Father is to share his very own life with us—the Son being one with the Father—enabling us to become his very children.

Through his life, death, and resurrection, Jesus reveals the love of the Father.

[Jesus], being in very nature God, did not consider equality with God something to be grasped, but made himself nothing, taking the very nature of a servant, being made in human likeness. And being found in appearance as a man, he humbled himself and became obedient to death—even death on a cross! (Phil. 2:5-8)

Jesus gives us the key to understanding the prodigal's return when he says, "for this son of mine was dead and is alive again" (Luke 15:24). All of our turning, repenting, and discovering the incredible love and mercy of the Father cannot bring us home apart from the redeeming work of Christ. It is because *he* was dead and was made alive again for us, that we can come to know the love of the Father and the way to the Father's house.

THE OLDER BROTHER'S STORY

I T IS THE CROSS of Christ that exposes the counterfeit love in which we as sons and daughters of Adam and Eve naturally live. How did the father respond when the older son's resentment and bitterness was exposed? He didn't say, "I'll give you a party, too," offering comfort to his son in his self-pity. The father knew that to give him what he wanted at that point would have been to support him in his sin. Rather, the father spoke the truth of the situation: "This [other] son of mine was dead and is alive again." "You are always with me, and everything I have is yours."

In hearing the truth, the older brother had the opportunity to recognize that he, too, was dead and needed to come to life. Blinded by his bitterness, he had lost sight of the value of the real inheritance that he had in his father's heart, in his father's embrace.

OUR STORY

I OPENED THIS CHAPTER with the observation that the one constant in the prodigal story was the father's love. Similarly, the one constant that makes the family of God a reality is the faithful love of the Father, and the related opportunities we have to come to our senses, repent, and receive the Father's embrace.

The Father's love requires freedom, maturity, and responsibility. It is a gift that moves in and through us as we cooperate with his Spirit. He calls us to return to him, not simply that we might be loved by the Father, but that we might reveal his love to his children and to the world. *When the prodigals come to their senses and remember the Father, will they find him in us?*

Committed relationships of love and intimacy with Jesus are gifts we receive, not things we can or should create. Our efforts must be toward **keeping** the unity of the Spirit, not creating it. "Make every effort to keep the unity of the Spirit through the bond of peace" (Eph. 4:3).

Genuine Christian community is our participation in the eternal love and unity of the Trinity—a share in the relationship of the Father, Son, and Holy Spirit. Such a community flows out of a vision of this love relationship. From this common vision is born a working together to keep the peace that has been given in Christ, to live the life that has been imparted to us by the Holy Spirit. Not everyone is called to participate in a family-type community, but we are all called into the body of Christ—called into relationships of love, in Christ. The same truth applies to us all: we are all called to reveal the Father's love.

I said earlier that the Father's love isn't based on need. Yet he has chosen, in a sense, to need us as unequal partners in the work of salvation. Not because he lacks anything, but in order to express his love in Christ more fully.

Over the years, you may have been hurt or bound up by controlling, manipulative relationships. If so, you may have a tendency now to want to be independent. But remember, **your freedom is in Christ.** I don't believe that seeking an independent lifestyle is the answer. Loving one another—being interdependent with other Christians as we are dependent on the Lord—is worth the risk of pain that can come from imperfect relationships. At the same time, I also acknowledge that human manipulation is so deceptive and deeply rooted that it is often best for someone to withdraw from a relationship for a time.

By the grace of God, the very conflict we face in Christian relationships often becomes the instrument to expose us to the love and mercy of God, the heart of the Father, his open arms of grace. At the point when things seem the darkest and least hopeful is often when our opportunity is the greatest.

Earlier in this chapter, I recounted the story of the Phantom of the Opera who had "passed the point of no return." The story didn't have to end that way. The grace was available for him to accept. But he chose to turn from it.

I often wonder: *Did the older brother remain in his bondage or did he, like his brother, come to his senses and return to his father?* I think Jesus left that question open for each of us to ponder. It's never too late to repent, and come home to the Father's heart.

9

The Repentant Heart:
Embracing the Father, Celebrating Life

WE ARE HERE TO CELEBRATE AND BE GLAD,
BECAUSE THIS BROTHER OF YOURS WAS DEAD AND
IS ALIVE AGAIN; HE WAS LOST AND IS FOUND.

— The father to the older brother

RECENTLY, I was sharing with a member of our community who had just returned from a conference on homosexuality. Ray noted that many people at the conference experienced very little understanding and compassion in their churches. They found all too frequently that the church was not a place where they could share their brokenness.

Happily, Ray's experience in our community over the past five years was quite different. He felt free to share about his struggles. He sensed that those with whom he shared treated him simply as a fellow sinner in need of Christ's saving power, not as someone who was fundamentally different, with whom they were unable to relate.

Several hours after sharing with Ray, I met with a woman who had left our community in 1982. Rachel's experience with us had been anything but life-giving. It had left her with much regret. While other factors could be considered, the main difference between her experience and Ray's was that in the intervening period of time, our community had gone through the process of repenting for being like the older brother. We had begun receiving the Father's heart.

Our time of repentance wasn't a decade spent in sackcloth. We didn't wallow in some morbid and unhealthy state of continuous mourning. Rather, we experienced the glorious process of returning to the Father and finding his love. God gave us repentance as a gift (Acts 5:31). It was God's kindness leading us to repentance (Rom. 2:4) and the gift of repentance leading to the knowledge of the truth (2 Tim. 2:25). We most fully experienced being his people when we stood together before the Lord in humility, brokenness, repentance, and gratitude, worshipping the One who had redeemed us.

As I look at our history as a community, the things that seem most significant are not the things *we* did together (although they were wonderful), but rather the things that *God* did among us. When the people of Israel were in the desert, they moved from place to place whenever the cloud moved. In a similar way, the most significant aspects of our life in community are found in the movement of the cloud of God's presence and in the fire of his purification. In the seasons of his judgment (an expression of his mercy) and in repentance, we have come to know who he is and who we really are in him.

JUDGMENT AND REPENTANCE

CHRISTIANS OFTEN look out at the world and say, "Boy, it's getting bad out there. God's judgment is going to come." But the truth is that judgment has already begun with the household of God. In fact, everywhere I've turned for the past several years, I've heard about different Christian groups, communities, churches, and individuals having a very hard time. "It's getting tough!"

My perception is that God has been judging his people. God is bringing about purity of heart. He's not interested in merely having us *look* good. He doesn't just want us to look Spirit-filled on the outside—he wants us to *be* Spirit-filled on the inside.

The Holy Spirit dwells and lives and moves in power, not only through us, but for us and in us to transform us. When God's judgment of sin becomes more evident and the crisis "hits our own neighborhood," God wants us to have his heart. He wants us to have the love of the Father. He wants us to love, not just by having a good program to help people out, but by being like him, loving others with the love of God. He wants the church to be prepared for what he's doing on the earth today.

Change within the church rests with the whole body, not solely with the leaders. Actually, my sense is that we often get the leadership in the body of Christ that reflects who we are. If we are more like the older brother, then our leaders will likely be like the older brother also. God, in his mercy, will allow this to produce repentance and brokenness in us, so we can come to desire the things that God desires. When it comes to repentance and taking responsibility for deception and unhealthy patterns, we all have a part. Leaders should repent in such a way that they fully accept the responsibility that is theirs, but also in a way that enables others to fulfill their part.

Most of this book has been spent talking about the sins of the heart—hidden, "underground" areas to which we can be spiritually blind. This spiritual blindness can be deeply rooted in our individual personalities, and in our corporate personalities as a community or church.

How do we pull up these roots? How do we repent? How do we return to the embrace of the Father and receive his heart as our own?

REPENTANCE BEGINS WITH REVELATION

AS I NOTED in Chapter 2, repentance—receiving the Father's heart—begins with the revelation of God's truth and love as well as our own deception. Only in the presence of light is darkness revealed. God's light reveals our darkness; his holiness reveals our corruption.

The first stage of repentance is the revelation of the truth. For me and for our community, that took time. We couldn't repent beyond what was revealed. I now see that this illustrates an important point about repentance: we need to pray for one another and be patient with one another, because conviction of sin is the work of the Holy Spirit.

God may have used this book to reveal truths to you. When speaking to us about the error of judging others, God used Jesus' words in Matthew 23. This is the kind of

Scripture I normally apply to other people! But this time, with the Spirit's help, I heard it for myself:

> *Woe to you, teachers of the law and Pharisees, you hypocrites!* [Yuck! That's for me, Lord?] *You clean the outside of the cup and dish, but inside they are full of greed and self-indulgence. Blind Pharisee! First clean the inside of the cup and dish, and then the outside also will be clean. Woe to you, teachers of the law and Pharisees, you hypocrites! You are like whitewashed tombs,* [Get the picture? Okay, join with me and listen to this for yourself—you'll love it!] *which look beautiful on the outside but on the inside are full of dead men's bones and everything unclean. In the same way, on the outside you appear to people as righteous but on the inside you are full of hypocrisy and wickedness.* (Matt. 23:25-28)

For years I had read this passage thinking about the Pharisees. People who lived two thousand years ago. Now, however, the power of the passage was released as I realized that God was speaking to me. May I invite you to read this passage again and ask the Holy Spirit to reveal its power to you?

Jesus says, "Blessed are the pure in heart, for they will see God" (Matt. 5:8). That Scripture doesn't just apply to the future; it applies right now. How are we going to see God in one another if we don't have pure hearts? How are we going to see God in our own lives or in the circumstances of our lives, if our hearts aren't pure? God wants to clean us out so our hearts are pure, so we can see him and know him. Only then can we really receive his love, love him in return, and have his love for others.

Only when we realize the truth that God is coming to clean up our lives from the inside out—that he really wants us to have a pure and a clean heart—can we then begin to submit in humility to what the Lord is teaching us about judgment, about pride, about legalism, about distorted love and unhealthy relationships.

It is one thing to modify the way we do something and to gain some level of internal change; it is another thing to be converted, to bring something to death and to find newness of life in the Lord.

Study alone won't produce conversion. Our primary need is for revelation. It is the truth that sets us free. As we ask God for wisdom, he will give it. When we seek his help, recognizing our individual and corporate dependence on him, he will expose deception by the light of his truth, and we will have an opportunity to respond to him and to repent in a deeper way.

REVELATION MAKES US COME TO OUR SENSES

"WHEN [the prodigal son] came to his senses, he said, 'How many of my father's hired men have food to spare, and here I am starving to death!'" (Luke 15:17). After willfully taking control of his life and squandering his good fortune, the young prodigal eventually got the picture. He "came to his senses." His hunger was met by the memory of his father, and he realized what a fool he had been. The consequence of his actions served him well. It revealed the deception he was under and he decided to return home.

The Scriptures speak of the hope "that God will grant repentance" and "knowledge of the truth" so that "they will come to their senses and escape from the trap of the devil, who has taken them captive to do his will" (2 Tim. 2:25-26). It is God's desire to grant repentance and knowledge of the truth to each of us. He wants us to come to our senses and realize the deception under which we have been walking, the trap we have fallen into, and who it is we have really been serving. Coming to our senses is the gift of God.

WHAT IS REPENTANCE?

WHEN THE HOLY SPIRIT is revealing something to us about who God is, the appropriate response is to repent. The Greek word for repentance is *metanoia,* which means to change one's mind.

Repentance involves changing your mind, purpose, or direction. It means selling what you have—that you might purchase the "pearl of great price." It means saying "No" to fleshly, selfish desires. It means turning from the way you are acting or thinking, and facing in a new direction. It means turning from sin, the devil's trap, and turning toward God. If sin is missing the mark, repentance is taking careful aim at the target.

Repentance is turning away from our former ways. It is saying "No" to our carnal desires. But it is much more than changing our old ways. It is turning toward God. It is turning toward what has been revealed by God, trusting in his love and his provision for our life and well-being. It means beginning a new life.

When our faith is weak, we tend to focus more on our sins, which we can so easily see, and fail to turn to God whom we find harder to see. When the vision of Christ and his redeeming work has been obscured, the prospect of repentance becomes an overwhelming burden. If the focus of repentance is on our sins alone, our efforts toward repentance become vulnerable to corruption by legalism, fear, condemnation, self-pity, self-focus and an unhealthy sense of unworthiness—all distorted, unsatisfying means for trying to meet the deep needs of our heart.

WILLPOWER ISN'T ENOUGH

THE FACT that there is a real need underlying our sin explains why it is so difficult to break the pattern of sin. The answer is not in simply turning from sin (which does not address the need) but in turning toward God who is the only one who meets our deepest need.

Willpower is involved in breaking with sin, but it is not the answer. The answer is found beyond willpower, beyond our resolve. Our "No" to sin *is* crucial to the process, but the answer is found in the love of God revealed in Christ, crucified for our sins. Willpower will help us say "No" for a short while, but it is our "Yes" to the love of God that will allow us to move into freedom. It is very hard to be good when we are trying to be good. Paul confessed, "I do not understand what I do. For what I want to do I do not do, but what I hate I do" (Rom. 7:15). If our focus is on doing or not doing, we are doomed to fail. A moral code is not enough to sustain a life.

We are created for relationship, not right behavior. It is in this higher call that we find victory and life. Paul continues,

"What a wretched man I am! Who will rescue me from this body of death? Thanks be to God—through Jesus Christ our Lord!" (Rom. 7:24-25). If we stop sinning and don't come to God to receive what we need through Jesus Christ, we are left with an empty void that must be filled. God invites us not merely to repent, but to repent, believe, and by faith find the One who gives life.

REPENTANCE LEADS TO FREEDOM

G OD-GIVEN REPENTANCE is not a burden; it is a gift that brings freedom. I've seen this time and time again. It was obvious in my relationship with my older sister. As I was willing to let go of my bitterness, I walked into freedom. It was true when, at the Signs and Wonders conference, I wept as the tenderness of God revealed how hard my heart had become. It was true in every area I held bound by judgments I had made of myself or others. God's revelation was the key to freedom. Repenting was turning the key to open the door to life.

It was clearly true when I first began following the Lord. I had felt threatened and insecure when I realized that my negative humor was not edifying to my new relationships. But I was afraid that if I stopped using negative humor, I wouldn't have anything to say! Yet as I repented and trusted him, I received new freedom to express my love to others. He gave me words of grace to replace my critical words disguised as humor.

The road to freedom is not an easy road, but it is the road of the Gospel. "For whoever wants to save his life will lose it, but whoever loses his life for me will find it" (Matt. 16:25).

When God calls you to lose your life, he calls you to give up all that you have become, all that you have made yourself, all the wisdom that you have accumulated from your experience of life apart from the knowledge of the love of God in Christ.

Even at Christ's birth we can see this theme of losing life to gain it. In the temple Simeon prophesied, "This child is destined to cause the falling and rising of many in Israel. . . . And a sword will pierce your own soul too" (Luke 2:34-35). If, in our journey, we ever decide that we are no longer willing to die—to our self-sufficiency and pride and control—we lose the power of the resurrection, which is ours only as we fall before our Lord.

REPENTANCE AND WORSHIP

A S WE WORSHIP GOD for who he is and leave behind the other things to which we are devoted, we grow in the freedom of the "new creation" we have become.

The object of repentance is not to become worthy; the object is to be more fully given to the One we love. That happens through worship. Actually, there is something circular about worshipping God. Repentance flows out of worship, and worship flows from repentance. As we draw near to God, the light of his revelation exposes our sins and brings us to a deeper humility and repentance before him. Then, as we turn from sin and continue to worship God, our repentance is made complete. When we are consumed with a sense of his presence, when our minds are filled with a vision of the glory of God revealed in Jesus, we are closest to our true identity—the person we have been created to be in Christ.

For most of my life I focused on the Lord's love for me, and I never considered my love for him as having any great value. How could my love and worship be of any benefit to the One who **is** love?

My wife has helped me answer this question. Several years ago she had one of her worst-ever migraine headaches. I took care of her responsibilities, got her the medicine, and sat with her, continuing to wonder what else I could possibly do to help her. But I missed the mark. None of these kindnesses was what she most wanted. Finally, she asked, "Could you just touch me, hold my hand?" (A little while later, a close female friend came to see her and started to touch her without having to be asked.)

In those painful hours, Janet meditated on the suffering of Jesus. The Spirit impressed upon her that as he hung on the cross, Jesus had no one to touch him in his sufferings. On our behalf, he experienced separation from his Father. Taking on our sin, he experienced the fullness of our alienation and separation. He hung suspended between earth and heaven, separated from both his Father and man, touched by no one.

Then Janet's thoughts went to the time when Jesus was at the home of Mary, Martha, and Lazarus. Mary poured a pint of expensive perfume over Jesus' feet and wiped them with her hair. This was extraordinary in many ways, one being that any woman who appeared in public with unbraided hair was considered immoral. Yet Mary wanted to demonstrate her love, to honor Jesus, to find a way of touching him, as he had touched her. She wanted to touch him personally. She could have used a towel but she used her hair. She came to him in humility; she did not presume upon him, she ministered to his feet.

Mary was foolishly extravagant, giving the very best, much more than necessary. The last time she had sat at his feet, she had been considered foolish in the eyes of her sister, yet Jesus had understood, saying that she had chosen the better portion. This time she would again risk being misunderstood by others. With Jesus, she could trust her heart and move without fear. This time, as before, she was criticized. Jesus came to her defense, "Leave her alone. . . . It was intended that she should save this perfume for the day of my burial. You will always have the poor among you, but you will not always have me" (John 12:7-8).

What Janet came to understand about this event was how much Jesus appreciated this intimate act of worship. The Scriptures tell us that the fragrance of her act—the fragrance of her love—filled the whole house. The perfume was a memory of her moment with Jesus.

WORSHIP AND INTIMACY

I NTIMACY WITH JESUS is the fragrance of our lives, communities, fellowships, and churches. The older brother in us doesn't understand Mary's action, just as the older brother in us is put off by the language of love and intimacy in the Song of Songs:

All night long on my bed I looked for the one my heart loves; I looked for him but did not find him. I will get up now and go about the city, through its streets and squares; I will search for the one my heart loves. So I looked for him but did not find him. (Song of Songs 3:1-3)

Intimacy was available to the older brother and to the prodigal. It is available to all. The Father's heart is open and vulnerable to his sons and daughters. He does not protect himself from rejection or hurt. How intimate the relationship is depends on the son or daughter. Intimacy is for those who want it, for those who realize their need, those who are in touch with their most basic hunger and thirst for God. How intimate we are with the Lord depends on how close we want to be with him.

There is something we have that Jesus wants. He wants our love, our devotion, our worship. He is looking for a place to rest, and he is looking to find a place to rest in you. He wants to touch you, and he wants you to touch him.

INTIMACY AND WELCOME

JESUS had the Father's heart. He loved being with his disciples, but his mission was always to the sick, the needy, the lost. It is a mission in which he invited his early disciples (and you and me) to participate.

Sinners loved to be with Jesus, because he loved to be with them. The Pharisees and teachers of the Law had great difficulty seeing the tax collectors and sinners gathered around Jesus. They indignantly muttered against him. "This man welcomes sinners and eats with them" (Luke 15:2). Jesus' response was to tell three parables: **the lost sheep,** (the good shepherd who after finding the one lost sheep invites his friends and neighbors to rejoice with him); **the**

lost coin (the woman who searches all over for the coin she lost and rejoices with her friends as she finds it); and, finally, **the lost son.** The central message is captured in Luke 15:7: *"I tell you that in the same way there will be more rejoicing in heaven over one sinner who repents than over ninety-nine righteous persons who do not need to repent."*

Jesus welcomed "sinners." He was attractive to them. He did not condemn them and label them as others did. Jesus looked at their hearts. He always embraced the humble and the needy, those who were honest about their condition. He had compassion for them, viewing them as lost. He met them on common ground. He didn't wait for them to come to the place of worship; he met them on the streets, at meals, and at parties. He was seen so frequently with the "wrong crowd" of his day that he was called a "glutton and a drunkard."

Jesus did not judge by outward appearances. He looked at the heart, knowing that the one who appears righteous may be much further from the truth.

As we draw into greater intimacy with God, our need for him is more fully revealed. Though we have been found, there is still a deep longing in our hearts. We long for heaven, our true home. This is the common ground where we can, like Jesus, meet and welcome the lost.

We often flee from the intensity of our longing. We flee from this longing by seeking to live a life in which we do not need to depend on God. We want to have enough possessions that we don't have to trust him for our provision. We seek to be good enough to have a right to heaven, rather than depend on his mercy. We seek to alleviate our longings through our attachments and addictions. We seek to make our home in the things of this world—which will never satisfy.

When we intensify our longing and dependence on God through humble prayer, fasting, almsgiving, and self-denial, we begin to move into the streets, the common ground where we meet others. It is out of this longing for the kingdom that we intercede, we serve, we work. It is as we realize our common longing and our common need that we can extend God's welcome to others and share the good news of the kingdom.

The message of the kingdom is good news to the humble. The kingdom of heaven is like a wedding banquet in which the invited guests do not come. The banquet is then filled by the poor and the needy, anyone who is found on the streets who will come (Matt. 22:1ff; Luke 14:15ff). The kingdom belongs to anyone who humbles himself as a little child (Matt. 18:3). It is as we identify with the poor and the needy, and experience in ourselves the transforming power of the kingdom, that we can bring a message of hope. It is then that our words about the kingdom have power to set the captives free.

When Jesus sent his disciples out to proclaim the message of the kingdom, he sent them out not simply to tell of the kingdom but to demonstrate the kingdom as they healed the sick. He did not send them merely to speak, but to give through both word and deed.

We are invited to participate in this "welcome home" that the Father is extending to those who seek him. Just as we can share in the Father's longing for his sons and daughters to return, we can share in his joy at their return. True celebration finds its source in heaven's joy: the celebration of life that God has freely given and freely redeemed.

Often during times of prayer, I find myself interceding for people or situations that I never planned to pray for. When I later learn how my prayer was answered, my joy is doubled. Not because I think my prayer alone was responsible for it, but because God allowed me to share in his purposes and give expression to his grace. When we give ourselves in prayer and service to others for the sake of Christ, we taste heaven's joy.

When the prodigal returned, the father ran to him and embraced him. He entered into a new relationship with his father, one of intimacy based on the father's mercy. It was now time to celebrate. "Quick! Bring the best robe and put it on him. Put a ring on his finger and sandals on his feet [all signs of position and acceptance]. Bring the fattened calf and kill it. Let's have a feast and celebrate. For this son of mine *was dead and is alive again;* he was lost and is found.' So they began to celebrate" (Luke 15:22-24, italics added).

All joy, all true celebration, is a celebration of life which finds its source in the resurrection of Jesus from the dead. Our joy is founded first in our return, the experience of his resurrection in our life. And that joy abounds as we participate in our Father's joy over other "lost sons" and "older brothers" who enter into life through the power of Jesus' resurrection from the dead.

Epilogue

YESTERDAY I RECEIVED a phone message that this book was going to be published. I had reread the manuscript last week, laboring without success to bring into it some of the fresh perspective that I've received through the refreshing grace of renewal that is touching people throughout the world.

Immediately after getting the phone call, I participated in a prayer meeting that, as it turned out, provided the "final word" of this book—expressed in the stories of three young people, Dan, Jessica, and Ed.

DAN'S HOMECOMING

DAN, A 24-YEAR-OLD MAN who had grown up in our community, felt compelled that Sunday evening to share his story with us. It is a story we all knew but had never heard from him. In his own words, it was a "near death experience."

When Dan went away to college, he embarked on a way of life that he knew was not pleasing to the Lord. It was a life filled with partying, drinking and immorality. Eventually he dropped out of school, and moved in with his girlfriend. He had made his choice and was captured by it.

Dan had grown up in a Christian home, heard the gospel message, received the sacraments and training as a Catholic, and experienced God's presence at various times in his life. But he never knew what it meant to be rescued by Jesus. Now came the moment of truth. The presence of God was just a fading memory, but also a gnawing one, exposing his inner death. For the first time in his life, Dan felt isolated from his father. His Dad, who had been so much a part of every aspect of his life, was now a distant figure. They were no longer able to even talk. The physical distance between them of 300 miles reflected the emotional and spiritual distance Dan felt. A sense of abandonment left him lonely and depressed, with thoughts of suicide. His body gave way to mononucleosis and hepatitis. With no health insurance, Dan's only choice was to head home.

Arriving at 30th Street Station in Philadelphia, he was filled with anxiety. If he encountered his father's judgment and criticism, Dan would have absolutely nothing to say, no defense, no excuses.

As he stepped off the train, his Dad saw him first and approached him with an embrace of love and acceptance. Dan heard no accusation, no criticism. He was welcomed home.

Through God's grace at work in his father's acceptance, Dan found his way home—first to his Dad, and then to his Lord. It was a struggle, but he made it, and eventually married a wonderful Christian woman named Donna. Dan now knows Jesus in a new way; as one who realizes how very close to eternal death he was, he has a deep appreciation of his merciful Savior.

During his wandering, Dan was attending a university known for its Christian orthodoxy and atmosphere. He had the comfort of being surrounded by "good" people. In a recent conversation with his wife, Dan wondered, "How is it that I can talk to my college friends about our wayward lifestyle at the university and they appear to feel fine about it? I never really felt fine about it."

"It's because," Donna responded insightfully, "you had tasted of something better. You couldn't be satisfied with anything less."

Dan's story touched our hearts deeply. Here was a "son" who had tasted of the kingdom growing up amongst us. Now he was expressing his deep gratitude to us for welcoming him home, confirming for him the love and acceptance of God.

His story is that of the prodigal come home.

JESSICA'S AWAKENING

DURING THAT SAME MEETING, I also had a chance to speak to Jessica, an 18-year-old member of our community. From all appearances, she is as sweet and as "good" a young person as you would ever want to meet. She loves God and wants to serve him. But lately for her it has been a time of crisis, a time of realizing that her life is a mess.

Yes, Jessica loves God, but she discovered that she doesn't want to take the risk of serving him, the risk of failing. She has served in safe situations, as part of her family and with friends. Now, with an opportunity to step out on her own to help some other young people, she has found it to be a time of anxiety, confusion, unruly emotion and self-centered worry.

As she shared her inner struggle, it was clear to me that she was facing the ugliness within. I rejoiced at this moment of grace.

It was a moment for an "older brother" to return, a time to realize that apart from God her life really is a mess. Deep down, she is really no different than the prodigal who more flagrantly went his own way. Jessica's idol is to succeed at being good, to be liked, to be safe, to be known as someone who loves God—and to do it herself, not having to be desperately dependent on God's grace. By his grace, she now has an opportunity to understand—without going the way of the prodigal—her need for Jesus and that he did indeed save her as well.

ED'S REFRESHING

A LSO AT THE PRAYER MEETING was a man whom I had met fifteen years ago, when he was a freshman at Villanova University. Several years ago Ed entered seminary, following a call to serve the Lord as a priest.

At one point in our meeting, I spoke about a specific sense I had that God wanted to touch someone who was experiencing a ball of mixed up and confused emotions. Afterwards, Ed came to me saying that he believed God had spoken to him through what I had shared; he wanted to pray together about it.

As we prayed, it became evident that God was indeed touching him. What came to his mind was a nagging, recurring thought that he, like Moses, would come right to the edge of the promised land but would never be allowed to enter.

I prayed a very simple prayer, "Lord, Ed has been hearing 'No' for a long time, and I believe you want to say 'Yes' to him."

Since this was such a deeply rooted struggle in his life, Ed expected to go through a lengthy process of prayer and interchange. He was waiting for more. Yet it appeared to me that the Lord had already touched him. God's purposes were already accomplished through that brief prayer.

The grace of God was there for Ed to face the lie. He had confessed it, and that simple prayer was all that was really needed. I said, "Ed, you don't need to go through a long psychological process to receive. Just receive."

At that point, he began to laugh. And he laughed for a good ten minutes, saying over and over again, "It can't be so easy. It can't be so easy." In that moment of grace, Ed's heart was connected with his Father in heaven once again.

The significance of this event, Ed testified, was that it exposed the stronghold of intellectual pride in his life. His laughter broke it as he prayed within, "Lord, let me understand less, so I might know you more."

Ed is blessed with a tremendous mind, which I am sure God will continue to use for his glory. But he was now saying, "Lord, I no longer want to find my life through my intellectual ability, but through my relationship with you."

Ed's final prayer was an expression of awe at the mercy of God. God had broken the rules. He had touched him and set him free *before* he had prayed a prayer of repentance.

Ed had received the grace of repentance, turning away from sin and toward God. And it had taken place in such a way that he was humbled by the power of God's grace. He had opened the door just a crack and the Father, filled with compassion for him, ran to him, threw his arms around him and kissed him. The touch of God had set him free. Now he was called to walk in this freedom and sin no more.

FINAL REFLECTIONS

OVER THE LAST YEAR I've had the opportunity to see many like Ed and Jessica return to the Father's arms as "older brothers," entering again into intimacy, finding refreshment and renewal in his presence. I have witnessed others who, like me, have walked a long road of return and are now experiencing the Father's embrace and his call to "let the celebration begin."

With this new season of renewal, I can now end this chapter in my life and this book about the older brother by offering two final reflections.

Firstly, the prayer of Psalm 51:12 is being answered: *Restore to me the joy of your salvation.* Joy is returning to those who have labored, remained faithful, and, at the same time, have been willing to humble themselves and face the condition of their hearts. With greater faith and assurance than at anytime in the last ten years I can say to you: *God is ready to touch you and restore your joy.* It may be as simple as praying with someone a brief prayer, similar to the way I prayed with Ed, and letting God touch you and restore your joy.

Finally, I posed a question in the first chapter, asking what might have happened if the prodigal had been greeted by the older brother instead of the father. More than ever before, I believe God is doing something wonderful to transform the older brothers—in preparation for a long awaited time of evangelism that will bring home many Dan's. In the days ahead, we will see a great harvest of prodigals—who return and find in the church not the heart of the older brother, but the heart of the Father.

WE ARE HERE TO CELEBRATE AND BE GLAD, BECAUSE THIS BROTHER OF YOURS WAS DEAD AND IS ALIVE AGAIN; HE WAS LOST AND IS FOUND.

— The father to the older brother

Acknowledgments

So Sarah laughed . . .

— Genesis 18:12

W HEN THE IDEA of writing a book was first presented
to me, I laughed. It seemed totally preposterous. Just
as the aging Sarah felt that it was simply beyond her capabil-
ity to bear a child, I felt incapable of producing a book.
Writing and English were never my strong suits in school, as
several teachers who struggled with me in their classes will
readily testify. And my inability to spell has become widely
known among all those who know me.

This book has become my Isaac, God's miraculous grace
at work in weakness, bringing to life what he has promised.
The promise was first spoken to me by Bobby Mearns, an
inspiring pastor from Ireland, who was a guest speaker at one
of our meetings. Bobby spoke prophetically that I would
write books.

Now, like Sarah, my initial laughter has turned to thanks-
giving and joy as I see the birth of an unlikely promise. I am
grateful to Bobby Mearns for his willingness to see something
in me and proclaim what was hidden.

I am also grateful to Ralph Martin, Fr. Mike Scanlan, Msgr. Thomas Herron, Trip Sinnott, Bert Ghezzi, Don Bartel, and Rick Joyner for taking the time to read and comment on the manuscript. Without their encouragement and steadfast belief in the value of this book, it may never have come to birth.

My heartfelt appreciation goes to Jay Miller, my lovely wife Janet, Evelyn Bence, Ann McKay, and Rosalind Moss for their devoted editorial work.

Nothing I have written has been in isolation. I am deeply grateful for being part of the body of Christ and for the diverse members God has raised up to nourish others. Among the many who have contributed to my growth and nourishment, I am particularly grateful to:

Ralph Martin, who taught me to pray through the first audio teaching tape I had ever heard, and who has faithfully stood by me in bringing this to publication;

Fr. Mike Scanlan, who was there to pray with me in 1970 and who has continued to be a source of inspiration and encouragement, as I have been truly privileged by our close, lifelong relationship;

Dave Nodar, a loyal and trusted friend who has always seemed to see more in me than I do;

John Wimber, for just being himself;

My mother, Elizabeth Downey, whose love for the "amazing grace" at work in her life has been for me a constant source of help and encouragement;

My sons, Philip, David, Matthew, and Joseph—each a unique gift of God, through whom he has shown me my weakness and revealed to me his love;

And, especially, my wife Janet, who has been a faithful partner and source of strength and truth every step of the way.

I'm very thankful for my family, friends and members of the House of God's Light Community. Their names, though rarely mentioned in the text, are written into every page of this book. It is their love, patience and understanding that has seen me through as we traveled together through the time of discovering the older brother in our midst. What a privilege it has been to return together to the Father's house, to discover again "how good and pleasant it is when brothers live together in unity" (Psalm 133:1).

I feel privileged and grateful, too, for the opportunity to share with you some of what we have learned. I pray that you will seek to recognize the older brother in your own life and discover the joy of returning.

I am eternally grateful to the Lord Jesus, who reached out and snatched my life from darkness and revealed to me the light of life; and to the Father, who patiently and faithfully waits for the return of his children, and provides times of reconciliation and celebration.

Finally, I want to acknowledge and thank the Holy Spirit for providing a time of renewal and refreshment that is being experienced by many throughout the world. This book is the story of how we were prepared for this celebration. I believe, in many ways, this may be your story as well. The Father seems to be saying to many of his sons and daughters, *The older brother has returned. It is time to celebrate.*

About the Author

NEAL LOZANO has a master's degree in religious education from Villanova University, where he led an evangelistic outreach to college students for eighteen years. He has more than thirty years of pastoral experience helping people find freedom in Christ. Neal is the director of *Renewal and Reconciliation,* an association of churches in the greater Philadelphia region. He is also the senior coordinator of the *House of God's Light,* an interdenominational Christian community that he has pastored for thirty years.

A teacher and pastoral counselor for many years, Neal has led numerous seminars and has spoken at conferences internationally. He has also published articles, and written two books. This book, *THE OLDER BROTHER RETURNS,* has been translated into three different languages: Polish, Latvian, and Slovakian. His latest book, *UNBOUND,* is making an impact worldwide, helping Christians unveil God's plan for their lives.

Neal has recently served on outreach missions to Eastern Europe, Haiti, Turkey, Sudan, and Kenya, and has taught at the School of Evangelization and Christian Life in Poland, Latvia, Slovakia, and Ukraine.

Married since 1973, Neal and his wife Janet are partners in ministry, and have invitations for conferences all over the world. They have four sons, and two grandchildren.

If you would like to contact the author, please write:
NEAL LOZANO
HEART OF THE FATHER MINISTRIES
P.O. Box 905
Ardmore, PA 19003

E-mail: Neal@heartofthefather.com
Website: www.heartofthefather.com